What readers are saying about
Never Goodbye #GirlDad

"Candid, personal, loving, forgiving, sobering, and humbling. *Never Goodbye #GirlDad*, a beautifully-written memoir and a great testament to faith. One of the most inspiring books I've ever read."

-Dr. Max Soliguen, Pediatrician

"My good friend Hannah Joya, former Miss North San Diego, provides a passionately moving tribute to her late father Dr. Danny Joya. *Never Goodbye #GirlDad*, is an emotionally gripping and refreshingly honest account of a daughter's tender affection for her loving father. It is certain to provide healing salve for any who have witnessed the chronic suffering of a loved one. Laced with empathy for all who have ever been blindsided by grief, it is precisely what the good Doctor Joya, would have ordered! Hannah's buoyant and beautiful spirit etched in every page, drips with hope and compassion for all who suffer. Read it and be changed!"

- Dr. Daniel Klender, United States Navy Chaplain, author of *Living with the End in View*

"Authentic and transparent... Hannah has poured her heart, soul, and wisdom beyond her years through sharing her #GirlDad story and principles she learned along the way by revealing her deepest hurts and highest victories. We believe that Hannah's personal story in *Never Goodbye #GirlDad* can be a tool to uplift and inspire those who've experienced profound loss and turn it into a path they can step into for discovering their purpose and destiny that God has planned. As you read Hannah's story as we have, it is a vivid reminder of God's steadfast love, grace, forgiveness, and mercy."

-Phil & Connie Sanchez, Pastor of Saddleback Church of San Diego, Influencer & Podcast Host of *Convos with Con*

"Losing someone is hard but losing a parent is even harder. This book is a step by step journey of a father and daughter's love. It took me deep into the author's soul which unlocked all her joys and pain. This book taught me to live and love every moment... and to not take anyone or anything for granted."

-Marc Anthony Nicolas, Two-Time Emmy Award-Winning Senior Producer for *The Talk* on CBS

"Grief can take many forms and teach us lessons we never knew we needed to learn. It can show us the darkest parts of existence while at the same time, breathe life into the deep crevices of our intuitive souls. The beautiful bond between father and daughter in this gripping, real-life account of family trauma, teaches us the true value of unconditional love. It walks us down Hannah's unique path of energy, growth, struggle, and heart break; attributing her unwavering strength and perseverance to her forever guide, God. It reassures the reader that tenacity will get you far, but faith will get you further."

-Annalisa Sawick, author of *Vanilla & Sprinkles*

"Hannah Joya's incredible and deeply personal tribute to her Dad's courageous and faith filled life, *Never Goodbye #GirlDad* had me holding back tears many times, and that was just from reading the intro. Her family's journey touched me deeply on a personal level as my own Dad and husband, Dr James Lee both had significant health challenges as young fathers. It is also through faith and love of family that we were all able to survive and thrive. *Never Goodbye #GirlDad* is a poignant reminder to all of us that whatever challenges we are in, it is not the end of the story and that to heal, we must allow God to use our pain to uplift others. Hannah and her stories of love and everyday miracles truly exemplify that with God all things are possible, even healing unimaginable loss."

Dr Tess Mauricio, MD FAAD, Stanford Educated Dermatologist, Founder, M Beauty by Dr Tess Clinics, America's Favorite Dermatologist, author of *California Total Beauty*

"Hannah unfolds and refolds her story with an open, faithful and loving heart. She brings the reader into her dark, broken and painful times with grace, compassion, elegance and hope. Hannah's humility and humanity shine through, like her light which is the very essence of a life that also embraces joy, cheer, laughter and never-ending love. Hannah refers to those of us who read *Never Goodbye #GirlDad* as her friends. How blessed we are to be her friends."

Marilyn Tedesco, Rancho Santa Fe CA The GBS-CIDP Foundation, Board of Directors (2004-2018) Consultants to Management, Founder and Principal Consultant

"Hannah's story is honest and raw as it journeys through the highs of a true father-daughter friendship and the lows of losing her deepest love this side of heaven. Reliving some of these moments in reading Hannah's story is an honor to experience. It will strengthen your faith in times of doubt, and change your perspective as you face hardships in front of you."

-Chelcea Cummings, Owner of *LoveLight Paper*

"I had the privilege and honor knowing the Joya family when Hannah was still a little girl. I thought I knew the family well but reading her memoir *Never Goodbye #GirlDad* opens my eyes to a much deeper appreciation for the love, the sacrifice, the pain, the triumph, the hope, the despair, the resilience the whole family had went through for over 27 years. Hannah has the gift of chronicling such a life story in such an inspiring, poignant way. The emotion is raw, honest, heart wrenching. I found myself reading the whole manuscript nonstop over Father's Day weekend. Couldn't be a more fitting time! What a great way to pay tribute to your father. A must read for all!"

-Dr. Melanie H Duong, Sun Orthodontics

"Never Goodbye #GirlDad is a beautiful lovely well written memoir by the daughter Hannah Joya about love and resilience. I remember the first time meeting the Joya family at a patient meeting, Mary the wife of Danny Joya said she had to leave early to see after her husband who had chronic GBS/CIDP. As I learned more about Dr. Joya 's story, I was richly in lightened at his strength. Dr. Joya will always be known as the first recipient to receive the *Robert and Estelle Benson award."*

-Lizz Russell, Fashion Designer, CEO of the Lizz Russell Collection, 2x Author of *Smiling on the Inside*, Patient Advocate/ Liaison San Diego chapter of the GBS-CIDP Foundation

"From the first day I met Hannah I wanted to be her friend. Her vivacious personality, genuine love and bold faith makes anyone feel their worth. This book, *Never Goodbye #GirlDad* is no different. You will come away from these pages knowing your story matters and that trials and difficulties are a garden where the most beautiful things can grow. God always does exceedingly more than we could ever ask or imagine."

-Jacqui M.

NEVER GOODBYE

The Unbreakable Bond Between a
Dad and Daughter is Forever
#GIRLDAD

HANNAH JOYA

WESTBOW
PRESS®
A DIVISION OF THOMAS NELSON
& ZONDERVAN

WestBow Press books may be ordered through booksellers or by contacting:

WestBow Press
A Division of Thomas Nelson & Zondervan
1663 Liberty Drive
Bloomington, IN 47403
www.westbowpress.com
844-714-3454

ISBN: 978-1-6642-0286-3 (sc)
ISBN: 978-1-6642-0288-7 (hc)
ISBN: 978-1-6642-0287-0 (e)

Library of Congress Control Number: 2020916140

Print information available on the last page.

WestBow Press rev. date: 02/12/2021

Never Goodbye #GirlDad

This book is dedicated to my dad, the man who never stopped fighting. My iron man, my hero and my guardian angel. You reminded me that we aren't just here to be ordinary souls; we are called to be extraordinary.

So, this is for your remarkable soul; may no one forget your incredible love as we learn from your inspiring life. I can't wait for that day until I see you again in Paradise.

I love you Dad. *Mahal Kita*, always. Your forever princess daughter, Hannah.

Dr. Danny Joya
June 22,1954 – June 13,2018

Contents

#GirlDad Principle Five
Renewing Resilience

#GirlDad Principle Six
Learning to Trust in Him vs. Emotions

#GirlDad Principle Seven
Remembering His Love for You

#GirlDad Principle Eight
Setbacks Becoming Comebacks

WHAT IS LIFE?

That was the last text I received from my dad before he passed; before Heaven received the best gift that life could have given me. That day, I lost my hero, my best friend, my iron man. That day, I lost all faith in existence.

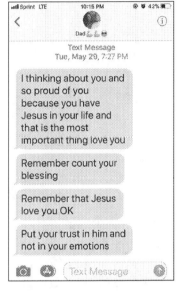

Why live anymore? How could I continue on with my life if he was my life? Death and grief do something to you; that was a day I will never forget.

The day I held his hand to my face, expecting it to be warm reassurance, but instead turning ice cold within seconds. The day I saw his body turn from white to blue. I couldn't even look at my dad's face when he was breathing his final breaths, because I was terrified to see what was happening. That day, I ran out of tears. That day, I lost me. That day, I cursed God's plan. Two people died that late afternoon on June 13, 2018, my dad and me.

Here today; gone tomorrow. The enemy used that day to break me, but in the end, you'll see that God used it to make me. Pain gives you two choices: it can make you or break you. You get to decide.

On that day, I watched my dad enter Heaven's gates right before my eyes and through that, I learned how to completely surrender.

What is life?

You may or may not have lost someone. Maybe your story sounds similar to mine. Maybe our grief, losses or heartaches in these next chapters are completely opposite or maybe they are perfect reflections of each other. Whatever your story is, we most likely have one thing in common; pain. Grief, pain and heartache don't discriminate. Whether you're twenty-seven or forty-seven, heck even eighty-seven, pain is pain. No matter if you went through a tragic accident and lost someone in five minutes or you lost someone over a span of five years, loss is loss; it's the same across all fronts. Don't compare traumas because it wasn't as long as someone else's. Pain isn't a competition, if it was, I certainly wouldn't want to be the winner. We all deserve recovery and support. The common denominator with everyone's story on loss, is pain.

I wasn't ready; he wasn't ready. No one is ever really ready for death. In this book, you will encounter and be a witness to my stories of pain, grief, depression, anxiety, loss and heart break that I have had to endure throughout my life. Without God's pursuing love, I would not have been able to get through any of it. With God, I was able to build resilience and see the lesson behind the struggle. Pastor Rick Warren states that there are six stages to grief: shock, sorrow, struggle, surrender, sanctification and service. I personally lived in shock, depression, PTSD and denial after the passing of my dad for one year straight; every single day and night. It wasn't until later on that I was able to trudge through the struggle. What I thought was the struggle initially, wasn't even close. At twenty-seven years old, losing my best friend, my dad, was the only thing I could focus on. As a family, we were challenged to get through all of that. In this book, I will tell you the ways that helped heal us as a family.

Are you in a season of perpetual negativity or feel your whole life has just been a broken record of sadness? Crying yourself to sleep has become your new normal. Not seeing the joy in life; simply not feeling much at all, has become your new routine. Depression has become a reality. Anxiety is everywhere you go. Waking up with dread in your heart knowing you somehow have to muster some energy for the day standing before you. Wishing a miracle would appear. Questioning your existence. You wonder, what really is life? Is it worth living? What is my purpose? If you've had any of those feelings or thoughts, you've picked up the right book, my new friend.

The encouragement that I have for you right now, wherever you are, at this very moment remember that this, this right here, right now, is *not* the final chapter. The impossible will become possible. You will be able to finish this book, you will take something from this moment, and you will end up choosing joy over sorrow. This is God's promise to us—He is close to those who are brokenhearted. I know what it feels like to self-isolate, to feel empty, to endure true tragedy.

While we journey through this book together, hold dear to your heart that your life has a purpose. No pain goes without purpose. You will forge through this tunnel and come out on the other side much stronger than you could've imagined. I will reignite the resilience that God has made ready for you, my new friend. I hope you don't mind me calling you "friend" throughout this book. You know it wasn't easy being vulnerable and writing my story, but through prayer, God made clear to me that someone—maybe that someone is you— needed to hear it. A story of a girl who overcame obstacles the enemy carefully placed in her path, forcing her to dig deep into her soul in order to discover the tenacity for life through God. These words I write won't bring my dad back, but they did bring me healing in the process. Not only are you going through a time of grief, heartache or loss, but I am as well. You are not alone. We are en route together, blooming in a new season of healing and growth. I'll say it again for the people in the back, *you are NOT alone!*

So, saying that, I hope you accept my invitation of friendship. It may come as a surprise to you, but since friends tell each other secrets…I was called "weird" my entire life. People would always say that I was too outgoing, too talkative, too hyper; they would say, "No one's going to want to be friends with you," so I tried to hide my personality. In fourth grade I began to be teased about my ethnicity. Being Korean, Filipino and Spanish, I would constantly get asked why my eyes were so small or why my face was so flat. Kids used to compare my face to a plate and make fun of the Asian snacks I would have at school. It got to the point that I was fearful no one would want to be friends with the "weirdo" so I ate my packed lunch of sushi and lumpia in the bathroom stall, alone. But one thing I was never insecure about was my dad's disability. It wasn't until I stopped caring what other people thought of me and decided to only care about what God saw in me, that I really started to gain confidence and realize my self-worth. The bondage of insecurity that chained me down no longer had a stronghold on my authentic self. God created us to be unique and special, so be exactly that; be you. Be the 'you' God designed you to be. I'm most definitely an extrovert, but at the same time, I enjoy being alone. I love reading and writing by my favorite candle, listening to some relaxing, soft tunes while sipping on a smooth cup of coffee. We are all special in our own way; don't let society or anyone tell you differently. If you still allow lies to rear their ugly face in your mind, God has the power to remove them. Stay strong, stand your ground, and do not allow those lies to have power over your life, let God. So now that you know a bit more about me, and you're going to learn quite a bit more as you read on, I think it's safe to say we are now officially friends.

Throughout this book I will share with you my raw organic truth; the life-transforming personal stories that were brought on through much pain and grief. Pain that became PTSD. Pain that seemed never-ending. Pain that appeared to be my final destiny.

Being born to a dad who was quadriplegic neck down from CIDP/GBS (Chronic inflammatory demyelinating polyneuropathy/Guillain-Barré syndrome) disease, a chronic illness that came with endless struggles in both my family life and personal life. The only vision I had of my dad, the only version I had ever known, was him confined to a wheelchair. I never had the privilege of seeing him walk, run, swim or dance, but that didn't stop me from living life to the fullest for my dad and eventually, for myself. For so long I was heartbroken, abused, betrayed, cheated on dozens of times in relationships and my dreams were swept away by rejection, after rejection. Despair was my middle name.

When my dad passed away in 2018, I thought that was my final chapter. End of story. What I didn't realize was that it was actually the beginning of a new life. Like a gemstone refined through tremendous pressure and heat, my new life began to take shape. God won't get you over it, He'll get you through it. By sharing my pain, I hope you too can realize that you can and will overcome difficulties, challenges, mountains, and fires. I'll tell you how it becomes possible to climb that mountain, to survive the trenches, and rise above what most would view as hopeless. Speaking truth with beauty beyond the ashes, I'll gently guide you back to God's love, who promises hope and a future, even when we don't believe it.

My mom's first child, my brother Mark, got to witness my dad go from a strong healthy person to being paralyzed from the neck down. Amidst this heart wrenching transition, my brother was truly a gift to my parents, which I'll speak more in depth about later on in the book. Twelve years after my brother, I was born into the world. My mom told people how I was such a blessing of laughter. My dad was so depressed, especially during the early stages of his illness, all he needed sometimes was to simply laugh. She would always say that God knew what he was doing by giving my dad a daughter at that exact time. Lord knows how many emotions surface when a girl is born into the family. Daughters have this special power in raising a dad's blood pressure and invoking a protective mannerism that no "man" can break without permission. But in all seriousness, the extraordinary bond between a solid father-daughter relationship is unbreakable. Being a dad is the most important role a man can have in his daughter's life. #GirlDad—the special loving bond between a dad and daughter that will live on forever.

The relationship between your parents is an entirely different bond, one that can serve as an example for honest love, if that is the type of relationship your parents had. As a young girl, I got to witness how my mom cared for my dad. She did all the tasks that most of us take for granted. I watched her feed him, brush his hair, change his clothes, and carry him to the car—things that seem so trivial and routine for most, but caring for your partner in that way is no easy endeavor, it's a labor of love. When my dad had to use the restroom at any time of the day, my mom would have to rush home and carry him from his wheelchair to his commode then wipe him and make sure he was thoroughly cleaned up before returning him to his wheelchair. Any person could perceive that kind of love as degrading or dehumanizing, but never for my dad. He saw it for exactly what it was, unconditional love. He never allowed those unique situations to damage his soul. Every morning and evening my brother and mom would stretch my dad's extremities which increased circulation in his body. We also had a stand-up machine they would strap him into so he could feel what it was like to stand again, even if it was only for 30 minutes. CIDP/GBS caused him to be in pain 24/7. My dad would describe the feeling as the tingling sensation you would get when your arm or foot fell asleep, except it was all over his body, *all* the time. I remember pinching my dad's arm and him reacting minutes later. Sitting in the living room and watching TV as a young girl, I recall my mom transferring my dad from the shower to their bedroom, water dripping everywhere, the dogs following close behind licking up each water droplet, and my dad glancing over at me while laughing. My mom was my dad's angel, my brother and I were my dad's little angels, and now my dad is our angel; our guardian angel. Our lives should surround acts of service because that's what God calls us to do. We are here to serve, not to be served.

What makes you happy? Genuinely happy? When we think of being happy, we usually think about getting things for ourselves such as status, fame, and fortune. When we take the focus off ourselves and focus on others, it allows us to see beyond what we think we might need. It allows us to see what God desires for our true happiness. The more we serve and the more we love, the more we will be blessed with genuine joy.

If you're feeling devoid of this joy; if you're feeling hopeless, discouraged, or depressed—whatever season you may be in where it seems like God has forgotten you—I'm so thankful that you grabbed this book to read. By the last chapter, you'll have a solid perspective on the healing power of God. You'll know how to embrace joy in the messiness of the unknown because in reality, life is all a mystery with a little thrill. But behind the unknown mystery is when God's loving hand works miracles and his true plan for you takes form. So, my prayer and hope is that through this new journey of healing you're entering in, you will feel the revival of God's refreshing love. If I can get through my darkest days, my friend, you can too. The book cover is a real-life image of me holding my dad's hand one last time at the hospital. The last promise I made to my dad was that I would never let his story of faith and resilience go untold. I promised to never let his pain go without purpose. Almost two years later, age twenty-nine, the promise I made has become a reality. You're reading it right now.

Buckle up friend, the season of vibrant, flourishing healing has begun.

> *"For I know the plans I have for you,"* declares the Lord, *"plans to prosper you and not to harm you, plans to give you hope and a future."*
> (JEREMIAH 29:11 NIV)

So, let's do this journey of life together my friend, the best is yet to come.

#GirlDad

Principle One

EMBRACING JOY IN
THE UNKNOWN

Chapter 1

Knight in Shining Armor

M any young girls have always dreamt about or were lucky enough to attend, the well-known father-daughter dance. Sweet, yet strong dads would show their little princesses how they should be treated and what it's like to be loved for the gifts that they were. I remember seeing the chivalrous acts of fathers from opening doors and presenting flowers to providing "piggy-back" rides and full on running jump-hugs to embrace their little gems in the excitement of the event.

Then, there was my dad. Sitting calmly in the passenger's side of his best friend's ride tryin' to holla' at me...I may or may not be listening to TLC as I write, ha. But for real, my mom would park in the reserved handicap area, I always knew where to find them, and my dad would be waiting for me patiently, ready for whatever adventure was about to come his way. I remember being so embarrassed sometimes, I'm ashamed to say, but I was also a kid and the reality of our situation was a far cry from most of my peers. Every time my friends would ride along in our van it was such an ordeal, finding a parking spot, pulling out the wheelchair ramp, unhooking the chair, making sure there was enough room between cars; we could never just pull in or take off. Nothing could ever be done in a hurry it was always a process. Even going out to dinner, I would have to call different restaurants to ensure they had certain accommodations. Nothing could ever be spur of the moment, everything had to be planned. Going to my Aunt's house required advanced notice so the ramp my uncle made was ready and waiting for Dad. There were no surprises, only advance notices. But I am not bitter at all, there may have been trying times throughout my childhood but in all honesty, I enjoyed the extra time with my family. It allowed us to embrace the present and as a family, more time together led to some fun adventures. Life is supposed to be adventurous my sweet friend, no time with our loved ones is ever wasted. Oh, how I desperately wish I could spend another hour with my dad.

I remember church services on Father's Day when the pastor would ask for all the dads to stand up so the congregation could acknowledge them. My dad was only able to raise his hand with the help of my mom. I remember people looking at me with pity, some whispering condolences that I didn't have a 'normal' dad. What is normal though? My normal was probably abnormal to most. But that didn't bother me. I didn't feel cheated out of a childhood at all. I never needed a dad to carry me or pick me up to take me to a dance. What I needed was a dad to show me, by his actions and through sacrifice, what unconditional love was. And my dad did that day in and day out; every extra second we spent rolling down a wheelchair ramp I began to understand what that looked like.

"There is no fear in love; but perfect love casts out fear."

(1 JOHN 4:18 NASB)

He taught me the importance of facing adversity head on and not being afraid of what's on the other side of the door when fear came knocking. He fought for his family every day and never backed down to a challenging situation. His courage taught me resilience. He was my "knight in shining armor" and would rescue me from any tower without a blink of an eye. His white horse may just be an electric wheelchair, but regardless, his electrifying "hot wheels" always did the trick. And instead of a "piggy-back" ride my sweet "iron man" would wheel himself outside to watch me walk to my car, I would look back with a sense of security and smile as he smiled back. Any time I looked back, I knew my dad would be right there. Whenever I would leave the room at the nursing facility, I would turn my head and wink at my dad, and I would see a warm, genuine smile grow across his face; in moments like those I knew I was ferociously loved. I would always say to him, "Mahal Kita" which meant, "I love you" in Tagalog. My father loved me beyond the "normal" and I knew that.

When things aren't the way we think they are supposed to be, we can easily go down the route of self-pity with comparisons. With social media being what it is today, we see everyone's highlights, everyone's most magical moments and it's easy to begin that comparison downward spiral. But we have to remember that everyone has struggles behind highlights; comparing steals joy. Through God's compassion and grace, we can have eyes that look beyond what we see right in front of us. God blessed me with a dad who wasn't able to walk with legs, instead, he "walked" by faith. I was taught things I would've never been able to learn if it wasn't for the illness with which he was diagnosed.

Friends, God will get you through so many situations and moments that help mold and create your character. Whatever abnormal or atypical situation you may be in, consider it a test. A test of faith. A test that will be rewarded. God sees your pain when no one else does. He sees your tears and hears your cries late at night behind closed doors. He acknowledges the pain behind the mascara cascading down your cheeks, He will always be by your side during those heartbreaking times. He is always there. You may not hear a booming voice or get an answer right away or in the way you'd like, but my friend, He will never leave your side.

Children crave love, nurture, attention and security from their parents. Maybe your own father or father-figure neglected you by choice. Or maybe you never even met your father, making that feeling completely foreign. Whatever your unique situation may be, remember that you have a "Dad" in Heaven. God is a dad who loves you and calls you by name. He is a dad who is always waiting for you to simply call out for his help. He made you, exactly the way you are, He loves you as His very own precious child. You are not an accident, no matter what anyone may say. You are valued in God's eyes. You were created in His image. You have purpose. Now dust off and straighten out that crown of beauty, your "Knight in Shining Armor" awaits you, my royal friend.

Chapter 2

Living Hope

Phil Wickham's song "Living Hope" is such a great tune. I listened to it every day in the hospital. It's one of the things that kept me going or at least allowed me to focus on things like lyrics instead of beeping machines. If there is one thing that's important to reflect on and worth restoring in your journey of healing, it's that there is hope. Hope to defeat grief, hope to overcome anxiety, hope to move through loss, addiction, depression, chronic illness, and hope to banish suicidal thoughts from your mind. There is always hope.

How do I know there's living hope you ask? I've seen hopeless moments in people who lost it all, and I mean ALL. Not just financial loss or the loss of material possessions, even though these can be major losses as well, but the loss of value and not just valuables. The loss of identity and purpose, that "what is life?!" kind of loss can be devastating to the core. It can bring a sense of hopelessness that only leads in one direction, a downward spiral into the abyss of depression.

Since the moment of my birth and throughout my childhood, into my teens and then during adulthood, I've spent so much time in hospitals and nursing homes that I have seen the rawness of hurt. The kind of hurt that seems so truly unbearable that one who has faith may even question out loud, "Why God?" and "Where are you God?" Which of course, only leads to hearts filled with confusion, doubt and bitterness. To this day, I still ask God those exact questions. Except the difference now is that when I ask, I understand that I may not always get the answer I want. There might not be a booming voice from the sky that says, "Hannah, here is the answer clear as day!" or a blatant sign that answers my question. Instead, I get my answers in knowing the truth in God's word.

This truth reassures us that God has a plan and it is a good one. We may not always see it at first and it may not go the way we want it to, I mean he never said life was going to be easy, but he will always provide us with a way. He will never abandon us, and He wants to see us succeed, not fail. He tells us 365 times in the Bible: DO NOT FEAR, one time for each day of the year. Our loving Shepherd will lead us along peaceful streams of flowing water, he wants us to have hope along our life path.

> *"Do not fear, for I have redeemed you; I have called you by name; you are Mine! When you pass through the waters, I will be with you; and through the rivers, they will not overflow you."*
>
> (ISAIAH 43:1-2 NASB)

Always acknowledge and be aware of the emotions you're experiencing, as you traverse this path. They aren't to be pushed to the side. Let them surface and if they've been hidden allow them to resurface, feel the realness of that true, raw emotion. Emotions are from God himself, but that doesn't mean we can use those emotions to make solid choices in our life. We unfortunately can't trust our emotions, but we can trust The One who designed them. We live in a broken world full of sin where emotions can create a detour and mislead our heart. People always associate emotions with heart, but they can be two separate things. If God is in your heart, then following your heart is not necessarily a bad thing and can be separate from what you feel emotionally. Place your trust in God himself; anchor your heart and mind in Him and you won't be able to drift away. Instead, you will find your heart beginning to align with your emotions as you become God centered, His emotions are without fault; a perfect design. As females, God designed us to be emotionally intelligent creatures. We are indeed more emotionally evolved than our counterparts, but that does come with a drawback….and that drawback happens to rear its ugly face about once a month. I don't know about you, but I'm definitely more emotional than usual at this time. So, words of wisdom to the fellas out there:

1. We are emotional, just embrace it.
2. Yes, PMS is real, no, do not reference it in an argument if you value your life.
3. Sweet cravings are 100% necessary so have a hidden stock to keep her happy.
4. God designed us this way and God's design is perfect (*insert wink, kiss face emoji).

Anyway, back to the most important lesson through all of this, hope. Despite my dad being told numerous times he may not survive another year after getting through twenty-seven years of paralysis, despite him being "tied up" to machines because of a tracheostomy so that he can breathe, despite all of these factors that he could not control, he still remained steadfast in his hope. That is the realness of hope. He didn't survive any of that because he was simply lucky, no that wasn't luck; he was thriving through hope. He was hopeful that God had a plan for him and there was a reason he was still here, despite everyone saying it wasn't possible. There will be times in your life, if you haven't experienced it already, when people will tell you it's just not possible for you to get through a situation, there's just no alternative, no choice as to what you're facing. I will tell you right now that there is always a choice. And I choose God.

> *"I can do all things through Christ who strengthens me."*
> (PHILIPPIANS 4:13 NKJV)

Here is what God wants you to do: show compassion with understanding and ignite the sparks of truth in your heart, know that God can and will overcome all. He is with you and will never leave you nor forsake you. When we are weak, HE is strong. HE has already won. You my friend, are clothed with His strength. Behind every pain comes with a purpose.

Chapter 3

Bitter or Better

We get to choose if we want to become bitter or get better. I have chosen both. I can truthfully tell you which one is worth choosing over the other, but inevitably, you need to experience one, in order to experience the other. Diamonds are formed in heat and high pressure; you don't get to see the beauty unless you walk through the pain.

I was so angry at myself for being bitter, being disappointed, confused, and angry at God. Having compassion towards others wasn't easy. We live in a time where altruism is difficult to come by; rare to find. Be the rare one. Trust me from experience, don't let this hostile world get the better of you and lead you away from your peaceful walk with God. I had zero compassion for myself and my lack of self-compassion, caused me to have none for those around me. Empathy wasn't even in my vocabulary at the time. I couldn't see beyond my own pain, let alone see the pain of those around me. Self-awareness is key and I was sadly, unaware. I was deceiving myself by thinking I was okay; that I was good. If I ever thought that someone around me was hurting, I would think to myself, how irrelevant it was. They didn't really know what pain, grief or loss felt like. They didn't have to experience what I did with a dad who was paralyzed for their entire life or experience someone cheating on them while their dad was dying in the hospital. While that may be true, they may not have had the *exact* same experiences I did, that doesn't give me any right to minimize their pain. We don't know someone else's struggle. Every situation is unique, and we are all on a different journey, even if our path's cross that doesn't mean we know their path. That's what makes this world unique. Pain is pain, there's just no comparison.

All those self-pity thoughts consumed my mind and were causing me to isolate myself from others. When you separate yourself from your lines of support, you open yourself up to a dangerous game. The enemy has you alone on his playground, playing by his rules. Jesus wants you to succeed, not fail, and He has given His believers the most important homework assignment of their lives. He wants us to teach others how to love so they may see God's love for them. Every single person you encounter is an opportunity for you to carry out that lesson. Whether it's your family, your friends, or even a complete stranger in the grocery store, whoever it may be, they are just as deserving of your love as the next person. We are not called to judge; we are called to love. Have the eyes to see people as God does; valuable.

My sweet friend, we are all given a story. Our story is to

be used as our testimony. Every person is deserving of love and never outgrows the need to be loved. Let God speak through your actions and your words. Surrender. Let go. Breathe. Inhale, exhale. Life can be so rewarding if we let it. Life can be so beautifully simple if we take out the complexities. Go out there with your strong, courageous, confident, beautiful soul and love on people. Don't let the world or events define your story, we have the freedom of choice. It's our decision to be bitter or get better.

I choose better...

#GirlDad

Principle Two

FINDING PURPOSE THROUGH THE PAIN

Chapter 4

Questions and Answers

Lysa TerKeurst author of the book, *It's Not Supposed to Be This Way,* stated accurately, "Though we can't predict or control or demand the outcome of our circumstances, we can know with great certainty we will be okay. Better than normal. We will be victorious because Jesus is victorious. And victorious people were never meant to settle for normal."

When my dad was hospitalized the last week before entering Heaven, there was a point early on that we felt hopeful. The doctors had told us that we would be out those doors in the next few days; he was expecting a full recovery from this recent bout of pneumonia and heart attack. I remember feeling so hopeful and grateful that he was getting out of this hospital once again. My iron man dad had defeated all odds yet again, HOORAY,

HOORAY! I started sending out thank you text messages to everyone who was praying. I posted on social media that he was on the road to recovery. Driving back to work I started praising God, singing out loud with my window down, just filled with so much happiness. My dad gets to continue to live in this life, I get to have my dad back. Two days later, that same doctor came back into the room with a different tone, with news we couldn't swallow or really process for that matter, "I'm sorry for the false hope, but there is nothing else we can do. His body is shutting down."

My dad passed away a few days after the doctor's announcement. I didn't really know who to be mad at. Mad at God? Mad at the physicians? What went wrong? What could we have done differently? Mad at my family? I just needed to be mad at something, someone, anything to distract me from the pain. That's the truth behind blaming and pointing fingers. It prolongs and numbs the real pain. It distorts, fogs and pollutes the mind from reality. My view on hope drastically changed after that week. How would I ever be hopeful again after experiencing such false hope? I inevitably became a negative Nancy. I lost hope in myself, I lost hope in life, I lost hope in having hope. Nothing was ever possible or ever going to work out for me. I wasn't someone you wanted to be around to say the least. Before all this, I always had so much optimism, empathy, faith and confidence anchored around my life. But after losing my dad, I was anchored down alright, but it wasn't to healthy things anymore; I was anchored down with grief, loss, depression, and pain. And above all else, I lost faith in God and His plan.

> *"Truly I tell you, if you have faith as small as a mustard seed, you can say to this mountain, 'Move*

from here to there,' and it will move. Nothing will be
impossible for you."

(MATTHEW 17:20 NIV)

My faith wasn't the size of any seed, it was obliterated. It
was nonexistent. That vibrant, healthy, full of life girl was a
thing of the past. Now I was a shell of the person I used to be.
When you go through something so hopeless in life, something
that is so completely out of your control, it's hard to ever believe
in hope again. How could I possibly believe that the best is yet
to come? How could I, right? How could the best be yet to
come when the worst just happened? My mind pulled a story
to the forefront of my thoughts, a very powerful story.

Billy Graham said it best in his online devotion, *Billy*
Graham Library on March 23, 2016: "The Cross tells us that
God understands our suffering, for He took it upon Himself
at the Cross all of our sins and all of our failures and all of
our sufferings. Our Lord, on that cross, asked the question,
'Why? My God, my God, why hast Thou forsaken me?' and
he received his answer, he knew. To redeem the world, to save
you and me from our sins, to give us assurance that if we died,
we're going to Heaven. He was saying from the cross, 'I love
you and I know the heartaches and the sorrows and the pain
that you feel.' Through the death of Jesus, came a grander more
magnificent gift. Forgiveness and eternal life. There is hope for
eternal life for Christ has conquered death. It also tells us that
God has triumphed over evil and death and hell. This is our
hope and it can be your hope as well. For the believer there
is hope beyond the grave, because Jesus Christ has opened the
door to Heaven for us by His death and resurrection."

The best is yet to come. Hope again. Believe again.

My dad was always hopeful, even as he opened his eyes

every morning and knew his situation, he remained steadfast in his hope. Every day when the clock hit 5 p.m., the love of his life, my sweet mom, would walk through the door after a full day of work and be by his side. Every single day for six years, she was there. She would walk through that nursing home, head held high, ready to serve. She was ready to help my dad along with any other resident who needed it; anyone who didn't have family to help them. My mom had the honor of holding hands with patients who were about to take their last breath without anyone else by their side. The nursing staff treated my mom as part of the nursing team because of all the help she provided for my dad over the years. Never a day missed. Never easy. My mom was there. My mom was always there. Not just for those six years where my dad had to be in a nursing home to get extra care, but also for the twenty-one years before that, where she was my dad's caregiver at our house. My dad was steadfast in his hope and my mom was steadfast in her love. She loved him for who he was, not because of what he had to offer her, but because of the vow they took the day they got married, and she never once looked at it as a hassle. Love is looking past the "Hollywood brand of love" and loving someone the way Jesus would want you to love; with kindness, holding no grudges, believing and seeing the best in people. For my mom, that meant looking past the disability and considering this marriage as her life's mission. Forgiving quickly and loving hard, in sickness and in health.

Despite my dad's pain, despite my pain in seeing my dad's pain, and despite the pain of the situation, there was always hope hiding somewhere nearby. And that next line of defense for love and hope besides my mom was my brother. My dad wasn't just a husband, father and friend, he was also blessed to be called a grandfather by my brother's three children: Joshua,

Addison and Gabe. Then, next in line for Joya defense, is ME! After my brother arrived "fashionably late" I popped right into my parent's world. During my dad's many years of struggling in and out of hospitals, I liked to find ways to brighten his day and help restore any lost hope. I always loved carrying big, oversized balloons that said, "Hey, Look at Me" to place in my dad's room, giving him a bit of comic relief. I absolutely loved filling his room with balloons. One time I brought balloons and told the entire staff it was his birthday (it was not…) and throughout the day amidst many birthday wishes and birthday songs, Dad and I had some good chuckles, despite his embarrassment at my antics. I did it out of humor and love. He knew that. At that time, my dad wasn't able to really move, so any type of laughter was welcome. We had a good laugh, always.

We hung out with my dad as a "solid squad," making the most of what we had. My loving aunts, uncles, cousins, and many good family friends would come with Asian food to make the nursing facility room feel more like "a home" for my dad. We celebrated dozens of authentic holidays and birthdays at that nursing home. We never needed fancy cars, fancy vacations, fancy homes or fancy rooms. We were never complaining and always laughing; enjoying the simplicity of it all. It didn't matter if it was the ICU or the nursing facility, as long as we had each other, we had everything we needed in Dad's room.

When we have something to look forward to, it naturally gives us hope. It engages those core beliefs that lead us to faith. Here is my hope for you, dear friend, that in whatever season and whatever challenge that may be causing you to halt, questioning God, "WHY?" I hope you can remember the grand finale. The grand finale of life. Within the pain try to see the light, the hope in knowing that one day we will see Jesus face to face. He will dry our eyes, wipe away every tear, and touch our heart; removing any pain we have ever known.

At that time, that "in the twinkle of an eye" moment when we have the privilege of being in God's presence and breathing eternal life, that is when all the hurt from life will be placed in His hand for us to see; for us to understand. His plan will make perfect sense. All the seemingly unanswered prayers and questions, the "Why did that have to happen?" or "Why did he hurt me?" along with the "Why did I have to go through that?" and "What was the point of that loss," all those will be answered as He gently lifts our chin and tells us how much we are loved by Him. With the devout angels by his side, the tranquility that is Heaven surrounding us, we will know the depth of his love. I imagine God opening the glistening, golden gates; I imagine them covered with pearls and fluorescent flowers, teaming with life. Stars bright, lions roaring, as Jesus speaks with a kind warm smile on His face.

> *"Well done, my good and faithful servant. You have been faithful in handling this small amount, so now I will give you many more responsibilities. Let's celebrate together!"*
>
> (MATTHEW 25:23 NLT)

Chapter 5

Sliding Doors of Life

One year and six months later: I'm sitting here with a messy, high-hair bun which has consumed way too much dry shampoo, an oversized sweatshirt that probably needs a good wash, and a half-eaten bar of chocolate while typing up this manuscript with a broken heart. Everything still feels completely shattered, the shock of my best friend, my dad, actually being gone—like really, really gone, is incomprehensible. I can't even begin to tell you how insane I thought I was becoming as I struggled with denial.

Denying the fact that I would never get to see him again, in person, on this earth. I couldn't listen to music for months because I'd feel guilting for being happy when I just went through such a monumental loss. I never said the word "dead" and I don't really say it now. That word is so final, so negative in my mind. To me, he is alive, but in spirit. I mean, I understood that he was no longer physically here, but understanding and accepting are two different things. I did not, *could not*, accept that he was no longer, physically here.

I was trying to fill this lonely place, this bottomless void in my heart that once was full of true purpose and unconditional love for my dad. A life enriched by organic joy was now empty and dark. When we search to fill a void, we end up looking in all the wrong places, and if there could be an award for finding all the wrong things to fill those empty spaces, I would've won it, ten times over. Every "void-filler" was different depending on my emotions. The one, or should I say ones, I always reverted to were broken souls. Those who didn't have Jesus and couldn't cope with their own demons; the ones who used verbal, physical and emotional abuse as a means to exert some control in their world of frustration. I figured that their words and their actions would forever define me. But let me tell you something my friend, God heals, and God has the final word on who you are, and you don't belong to *anyone* except for God. Don't ever forget that. You are the royal child He designed, and He can and will restore what was lost. So, let me save you some time and money on a psychologist by telling you this one, very important phrase: HURT PEOPLE, HURT PEOPLE. God is *LOVE* and Jesus saves. Find your fulfillment in the one who created love not in others.

For me, during those years, I was using the abuse to numb the real pain; my real feelings. Anything to distract me from reality. In those moments it was like an addiction, it was the "fix" I wanted, needed, and craved. I chose that over the truth because in my mind all other forms of pain paled in comparison to my grief. When you mix pain with loneliness and allow ungodly souls to fulfill your needs, you are on the enemy's playing field where he finds it easy to steal and destroy. We sometimes forget that our real enemy isn't actually people, it goes far beyond that, "the thief comes only to steal and kill and destroy; I have come that they may have life, and have it to the full."(John 10:10 NIV)

When we have so much instability around us, all we crave is stability. Friend, that kind of stability is ONLY found in God.

It seems so strange now as I reflect back on all those days of walking through the nursing facilities to visit my dad. I remember those moments when it seemed like such a burden to even walk through the sliding doors. Now, as I reminisce, it seems that we were actually walking into a refreshing environment. It was as though our souls were naturally craving it. We, as humans, designed by our maker, are naturally wired to receive genuine joy by helping others. When we walked into a facility with sick patients, we would feel renewed and revived, knowing that we were able to bring so much joy to those who needed it. And as soon as we left a facility, the monotony of our daily lives physically and emotionally drained us without even realizing it at the time. We were not made to live only for ourselves and our independent survival. We were not meant to be alone in this world. We are social beings and it's in our best interest, its hard wired into our godly souls, to help the survival of those around us. My dad's twenty-seven-year illness brought so much purpose to my family and I, and to everyone that saw us smiling through the pain. The beauty of pain is that there is purpose.

There is God's purpose. Trust me, there were days where I couldn't see it, days where I'd walk in so upset, but once I began to understand this underlying purpose, the truth of this life, I was awakened.

"Then you will know the truth, and the truth will set you free."

(JOHN 8:32 NIV)

God is close, very close to the brokenhearted. He longs and desires for us to call out to Him and He wants us to see the purpose behind the pain. Don't give up my friend, "just keep swimming" like Dory in Finding Nemo and have faith that it will work out in the end. Allow God's love to be your armor as you push through the pain. We may be wounded but those wounds tell our story and allow us to connect with others. So, in a sense, we are wonderfully wounded. And though it may seem to be contradictory, our wounds actually make us stronger. YOU ARE STRONG. We are wonderfully, wounded warriors with a purpose.

The beauty of pain is the purpose; it's the purpose you develop over time as you continue on living. It's the purpose that you can pass on to others who need it in their time of greatest pain. It's the purpose that grows in strength as you continue on, despite the enemy's attempt to destroy you. We could have easily walked through those doors at the hospital or nursing home each time complaining, grumbling and grunting, venting about our problems and pain, but we made the choice to follow God's example. There were days of complaining, but more often than not, we chose joy. And I say "chose joy" because joy does not come easily in difficult times, you have to choose it; you either get bitter or you get better and we chose better. I know it sounds crazy to say that we found a purpose in pain and learned to embrace the unknown through helping others, but it's the truth. People in the hospital would wonder, "Can you tell me why that family is laughing when they have someone so sick?" and I can tell you it was tough at times, but when you shift the focus outside of your own pain, it becomes much more meaningful to step through the sliding doors of life each day.

#GirlDad

Principle Three

TRANSFORMING TESTS TO TESTIMONIES

Chapter 6

Your Lease is Coming to an End

Life is short. The percentage of immortality is at 0%. We need to embrace life for what it is. However, with the reality of bills to pay and expectations, "life" gets lost amongst the "to dos" and the "to haves". Then, you keep hearing phrases like "YOLO" and "I'm getting old," "I should be traveling more," "you need to start planning for retirement," "prime years," and the list goes on. Just like we talked about earlier, comparing can wreak havoc on your mindset. When that kind of talk heats up, it's only normal to feel the pressure that comes with the brevity of life.

That was the beauty of Dad's journey. It allowed us to take

a bite out of life, that juicy prime rib we had, savor the taste and then look at the bigger picture of togetherness at the feast. It allowed us to take a step back and not get so cozy in the moment. It constantly switched our focus from the temporary pains and setbacks to a more eternal perspective; our future home, paradise, Heaven.

I had to go back to my dad's nursing home to gather his belongings the day after he passed. Walking through those doors, subconsciously thinking it was just another day hanging out with my dad. I was ready to see him right there in the courtyard getting some fresh air waiting for his family, but this time was different. He wasn't there. I wasn't ever going to see him again physically, on this earth. I walked into his room, fell on his bed and cried. I cried and cried, completely numb to everything going on around me. Despite crying, I felt I had no emotion, no feeling, I don't even remember the people coming into the room to hug me. I cried oceans of tears. To be honest I think I even fell asleep on the bed for a few minutes or maybe it was me blacking out from the shock. I didn't want to leave. I curled up in a ball and just laid there. Gazing at the ceiling with a blank stare. Hopeless. Lost. Confused. Angry. Bitter. Callus. "WHY GOD?" I remember saying aloud. The same room that was filled with so much life, family and love was now empty. There was so much more life left to experience with my dad. I was twenty-seven, ready to take on the world, my dad along for the ride, by my side, but now he's gone. And there I was, in the same bed my dad laid on for six years. I wonder what he thought about; what he prayed about. I left that day, walking the same halls, looking at the same walls, my dad's electric wheelchair next to me, just like it always was, except now my dad was walking beside me. My guardian angel.

I had a dream that following week, I was seeing everything

from my dad's point of view. I saw myself drive to the nursing home, gather his belongings, and cry. I'm not sure the true meaning or message behind that dream, but what I got out of it was that my dad was trying to tell me that I wasn't alone; I will never be alone.

Maybe you consider this earth as your last home or your last pit stop. There is a saying that in Heaven the waterfalls emit music with every crystal-filled raindrop; there is an endless supply of satisfaction and happiness. I don't know about you, but as good as french fries and pizza are here on this earth, an unlimited buffet sounds pretty awesome. Crystal-filled raindrops!? I mean, wow! Imagine the drip on that look! Our minds aren't even wired to grasp the beauty that awaits us.

> *"The twelve gates were twelve pearls: each individual gate was of one pearl. And the street of the city was pure gold, like transparent glass."*
> (REVELATION 21:21 NKJV)

I believe that God lets us know a little about Heaven, so we have a sense of always wanting more and never being genuinely satisfied with anything we're doing here on earth. Only in Heaven will our constant pursuit of happiness unravel.

Where do you want to spend eternity? It's not too late right now. Allow Jesus to purify your heart, His boundless love to consume you and His infinite power to lift your soul. Simply call out His name, breathe deep, inhale and exhale all the stress that dominates your life. Allow your shoulders to loosen up, smile knowing that God is faithful and has a plan. Laugh knowing that there is always light amidst the dark. Call an old friend where amends need to be made. Make a joke. Call your mom. Text your dad. Tell someone they're loved today. Our home is temporary, but what you do today matters most in your permanent home; it matters most to your eternal soul as you are lifted through the heavenly gates. Grief became more manageable as I was comforted in knowing that one day all my sadness will disappear. I know where I am headed, where my dad is now; a new resident in Heaven. Life on earth is like an apartment, and your lease will eventually come to an end.

So today, my sweet friend, I pray and hope that you will allow God to refresh your mind from whatever is stealing your happiness. Open your heart to His unfailing love. Nothing on this earth is permanent except your salvation; your personal belief in Jesus Christ and that he died for your sin. Your lease for your temporary home, your physical being, is coming to an end every single day your lungs breathe and heart beats. How's your temporary home looking? Is it messy, sad, and filled with anxiety? Be sure that when the Landlord comes to check you out, you're ready.

Chapter 7

Field Trip

At some point in our lives most of us have experienced a field trip, a class outing or a vacation with the family, even an errand to the grocery store. We've all been on our own version of a field trip. Due to my dad's severe disability, our trips were always unique.

As a young girl, I took weekly field trips to the ICU hospitals. On days where my mom was unable to drive us for the weekly clinic visits, I got to take a ride on a special shuttle bus that catered to the disabled. I thought it was so fancy and cool to see all those people wearing white "robes" (medical doctors) and I remember people taking field trips to our house (the in-home nurses that gave my dad IV infusions). As I got older, the field trips became more frequent. I learned to make the most out of these situations by finding the best coffee carts at each hospital we went to and looking forward to eating out at the yummy cafeterias with my mom. I would always get excited at the different views from each inpatient room my dad was admitted to. I would enjoy new shows and episodes on the TV at each facility while waiting for the doctors to give us the "news of the day" regarding my dad's health.

Miracles are everywhere. Just because an incident occurs that doesn't align with your plans does not mean that a miracle isn't present. I have told myself many times that I will refuse to see my dad's passing as a failed miracle. My family and I continue to experience miracles everywhere, large and small. You just have to be open to seeing them, which is not always easy to do. Finding a miracle in a test, can sometimes be like finding a needle in a haystack, but the needle *is* there.

Every month for twenty-seven years we had a funeral planned out. Because of my dad's delicate state, getting the flu or pneumonia could mean death, and unfortunately, my dad would get sick often. We were repeatedly told that he "wasn't going to make it" and I had to say my "goodbye" dozens of times. Mentally, that did something to me. That mentally tested my resilience. We were always prepared for the worst and hoping for the best, which sounds so cliché but it's so true. God wasn't finished with my dad yet…miracle after miracle… the power of prayer. Many times, my dad's physicians were perplexed as to why he was able to make it through some illness or ordeal; they couldn't comprehend how my dad had come out on the other side of these "near death" episodes.

With each test, prayer always won. With each test, family always won. And with each triumph and each miracle, we always came out on the other side laughing. We would laugh in the face of fear because without humor, what is life? I will never forget one such occasion, since we are talking about trips and family outings being unique…fear was definitely involved for those in close range, ha. Whenever we would attend any function, we would always bring a urinal for Dad. Between my mom, brother and I, we would have to assist him in using this portable restroom. It was never really a quick trip, I mean nothing was ever quick, but because of the lack of muscle, we would sometimes wait for fifteen minutes before my dad was able to go. Any "normal" person would have probably been embarrassed or mortified on these occasions, but then again, my dad was far from normal and I think he began to rub off on the rest of us. While my mom was removing the urinal, thinking he was finished, my dad's body decided he wasn't. It was not the first, nor was it the last time that the urinal was frantically returned to its rightful place amid pee flying everywhere, with screams and laughter following close behind. We were always making light of things, without that, I don't think most of us would have gotten through the day to day. We saw the "miracles" where most would not.

Another one of my favorite "Dad miracles," was the time he had a roommate at the nursing facility, Mr. Lynch. I remember meeting him for the first time. He ushered me over to a picture of his wife on the wall, reminiscing about how beautiful she was with a smile on his face. He would begin to tell stories of the four amazing boys they raised together while my father and I patiently sat on the bed listening. Mr. Lynch was an honorable Veteran who had served the U.S. in the Korean War. My dad and him used to play "battlefield," each pretending to dodge bullets left and right. Besides being goofballs, they looked out for each other. If one of them needed the nurse and couldn't reach the call light, the other would ring the bell. Holidays were no exception and there were so many "miracle" moments we got to experience with each other. I remember one thanksgiving in particular. The church we attended had a holiday program where you could adopt two active duty military men for the day, since they were unable to be with their families. We always participated, welcoming them into our home, thanking them for their service and introducing them to some good ol' thanksgiving food. One year we decided to bring the guys to visit Mr. Lynch at the nursing facility. It was such a special moment to see these two young men honor Mr. Lynch by saluting him. He quickly became part of the family. Becky, Mr. Lynch's daughter-in-law, would always help decorate their room for the holidays. My mom and I even had the honor of attending the wedding for Darren (Mr. Lynch's son) and Becky, who always checked in on the two. We never worried when we left Dad, knowing that Mr. Lynch was there to watch over him. My dad was there when Mr. Lynch took his final breath; even as he entered Heaven's gates, he was not alone.

Whether it's the end of your trip or the beginning, everyone's life trip is different. That in and of itself is a miracle; it makes you unique and special. Talk about your adventures, your field trips, your family outings, your laughs and don't be so serious. Allow God's love to pour over you and embrace each miracle moment for what it is. And when you fall down, get back up and continue on. Don't let this life trip you up or you'll miss the miraculous miracles designed to be discovered.

Chapter 8

Sweet Dreams, Mom

Not only did I grow up being raised by a dad who was physically paralyzed my entire life but I spent every day of my prime years (22-27 years old) in nursing homes and hospitals. Those years were meant to be times of growth, new relationships, career changes, traveling and so forth. My prime years were not just a superficial season, they were unique and special because I learned firsthand, how to depend on God's plan over mine. Trying to force your plans because of age or society will cause you to become stressed and depressed. If you trust in God alone to direct your path, it may look narrow, but I assure you, it'll be worth it when you reach the destination. I'm thankful that during my prime years I had to face the hardest of challenges because it led me into some amazing friendships. There's always a silver lining.

Our family started a nursing home ministry. Every Sunday we would hold a church service at the facility for any residents that wished to come. We found that there were actually many residents who had no family members that came to visit them. They might have piles of stuffed animals and a poster board with a small compilation of pictures, but no family present.

I believe God placed us at specific nursing homes, at specific times, to show our love to specific residents, who needed someone at that, specific moment. Not only did we get to experience some of the best ministries with sharing God's word, but we were also blessed with laughter. So many residents just needed to laugh and honestly, so did we. Laughter can do wonders for the soul, especially in places like nursing homes. I made a comment to my mom once about how interesting it was that we come into this world as sweet, naïve little children, and then, as older adults, it seems we become children yet again. It seems they have rediscovered their inner child in their final days. Life comes full circle. If you haven't ever made a visit to a nursing home, you are overdue my friend and you're missing out! I have never received so many blessings, compliments, and overall appreciation for simply smiling, singing to them, and being present. I not only built strong bonds with each resident; they became my extended family. Your companionship could mean the world to a resident and I promise, you'll gain some new muscles in your face from smiling so much.

My mom, being the angel she is, started another nursing home ministry by herself. Her ministry consisted of her going from room to room, making sure all the patients had enough blankets and everything they needed. She would often cover them up, tuck them in and whisper "sweet dreams." She was the voice for those who were, or felt, voiceless.

Resident care within nursing homes was very questionable for the most part and was often times a case of total neglect. If my family had not been there to watch over my dad 24/7, he probably wouldn't have lived as long as he did. Too many nursing home patients are experiencing elder abuse. Just look it up on the internet, there are so many instances. It's **real** and it's **wrong**. A change needs to be made and awareness is essential. Patient care needs to be a top priority anywhere and everywhere. I would always tell staff to treat patients the way they'd want their family member to be treated; with love, compassion, patience and grace. Don't get me wrong, we have had some outstanding patient care at certain facilities. So much so, that we still remain friends with some of the staff and physicians that cared for my father. The bible teaches us how to care for others.

> *"Truly I tell you, whatever you did for one of the least*
> *of these brothers and sisters of mine, you did for me."*
> (MATTHEW 25:40 NIV)

I just want to let others know that neglect and elder abuse do exist and it's important to know what's going on wherever your loved one resides. I encourage you to please, PLEASE, make regular visitations to your local resident homes. Just go love on them. Listen to the stories they want to tell you. Allow their voices to be heard. Bring your dog as pet therapy. Bring your children; they love kids. Share a little cheer with some songs. Ask if they need anything or how you can help them. But do it with a pure heart, seeking no glorification. God sees your heart; he sees your actions and that's all that matters.

My mom never sought praise for all that she did, it came

from the bottom of her heart. She would always say that she's "the only Jesus that these people would see."

We built so many relationships at every facility and all those special bonds are held close to our hearts. Unfortunately, as time passed, we watched a lot of those new friends pass away, just like Mr. Lynch. I could fill a novel with all the residents with whom we bonded. But right now, I'd like to share about two other sweet, very special souls.

One such sweet bond was with a woman who we'll call, Justine. She is an angel now. Justine had a very severe stroke at a young age. She never married and never had children. She told me that she could have been a pro bowler. At times when my dad was having his bath, I would mosey on down to Justine's room. She would always appreciate the time I spent with her. She once told me I was her only friend because she didn't like anyone else at the nursing home. She would join our family parties whenever we hosted them, and we always gave her a slice of pizza.

One evening, I was completely exhausted and on the verge of delirium; it was about twelve a.m. Justine was still up and I was pushing her back to her room when we smacked into the wall. I hadn't realized just how hard I was pushing her wheelchair. Her hands went up in the air as if she was on a Disney roller coaster ride. Justine had, in that short time, surrendered to her inner child. She and I stood there for a second and then busted out laughing like little troublemakers goofing off. Forgetting for a moment, the reality of our situations, forgetting the severity of her condition, forgetting the sadness surrounding disease, forgetting, just for a second, where we were.

Due to the severity of her stroke, Justine's speech was slurred, and she was difficult to understand. But words didn't need to be exchanged between us, we had a special connection.

Maybe it was the way she looked at me when I spoke or how we listened to each other. Or maybe it was the endless number of snacks she had in her drawer which she offered me daily. Whatever it was, we just knew what the other needed. She even called me once on the Fourth of July, randomly asking how I was. That will always stick with me. Love that girl.

Another beautiful soul we bonded with was Victoria, or so we'll call her for the sake of confidentiality. No one ever came to visit her. Victoria struggled with a very severe case of dementia. She had once been a beloved wife and sister but had since been forgotten by her family. She would always be waiting in the nursing home foyer, clinging to her stuffed animal and chomping on her bubble gum while she greeted people, just like my dad. She and my mom shared a very special connection. On Mother's Day one year, I asked my mom what she wanted to do since it was her day. She said that the best way to celebrate Mother's Day would be to take Victoria out for lunch. So, we did just that. With the nursing staff's permission, we got to take Victoria to a historic steakhouse right down the street. That was the first time Victoria had gone out in fifteen years! And I'm not saying "gone out" as in, went to a restaurant, I mean OUT, like *outside*! Victoria was afraid of the sun and needed 24/7 supervision if she were to go outside due to her mental state. Friends, I don't know about you or if I'm alone on this, but if I don't go outside at least once a day to get some fresh air, I will legit go insane. Imagine fifteen years of being stuck inside. That's the difficult truth for some of these residents, it's too much of a hassle for everyone, so they stay inside for the remainder of their life.

During her last week here on earth, it was evident that Victoria would be taking her final breath soon. She had been placed in palliative care, which means they try to provide as much comfort as possible to the resident during their final stages. Just before we were to leave the nursing home that night, my mom went to visit Victoria alone. She had been unconscious for days. My mom gently held Victoria's hand, repeating the Lord's prayer to her. My mom told Victoria how much she was loved and walked away. As she was turning to leave, Victoria opened her eyes, looked at my mom and said, "Mary, I love you." She closed her eyes and entered Heaven's gate the following hour. My mom and Victoria will have a sweet reunion in Heaven one day.

God used my mom to be a friend to Victoria in her time of need. God used our family to provide love and laughter for Justine. God will use us for good if we are open to his plan. He will use our trials and convert them into testimonies so others can see the joy amongst despair. God intentionally places people into our lives. Love them. Encourage them. Pray for them. Show them they are valued and seen. Never take any moment for granted.

Everyone in your life is there for a reason. Allow God's love to show you how you can bring peace to others. We are God's ambassadors. Let's live with that truth.

Victoria and Justine, we love you. Live it up in paradise and give my dad a big ol' hug from his Princess.

Chapter 9

Shoulda, Coulda, Woulda

I had so many regrets after my dad passed. So many, that I could probably write another book on top of this one, just filled with my "shoulda, coulda, wouldas." There is one in particular that weighs heavy on my heart, one that I'll share with you my friend, not because this moment could have been recognized and changed, but because this moment has reminded me a lot about forgiveness. This test reminded me that I easily forgive others, but forgiving myself is much, much more difficult.

I actually graduated as a respiratory therapist believe it or not. Ironic how life does that to you sometimes. It was crazy and amazing to realize that a lot of those who taught me, were now the same respiratory therapists who were taking care of my dad. As much as I thought the medical field and helping people was my calling, I was being pulled toward a very different path. In early 2018, not knowing that within a few months my dad would no longer be with me, I had decided to move to Los Angeles to pursue a modeling and acting career. My dad was never fond of me being in that industry. How was I to know that same year was his last year? We had prepared for his "last" moments so often, how could I have known that this was *actually* going to be the last? I would've never moved.

One day, while I was living in L.A., I was so sad and upset after receiving news that I didn't get a part I had auditioned for when my phone suddenly pinged. Now, my dad had this weird sixth sense for knowing when I needed encouragement and a laugh. His dad radar must've been going off that evening because I definitely needed him. At the time, he was staying in a nursing home and had used his call light to make it seem like he urgently needed assistance from one of the CNAs (certified nursing assistant) on duty. When the CNA answered his call, my dad asked her to grab his phone. The CNA initially thought he was wanting to call my mom, as he would call her at least sevhisen or eight times a day, but with his scratchy voice he said, "Snaa ... Snaaa ... Snaaa..." The CNA immediately called other nurses into the room thinking that my dad may be having a heart attack or stroke. Just then, my dad used more muscles than he had in a long time and screamed out, "Snapchat!" causing quite the commotion. My dad made the nurses create a Snapchat account and insisted they find the "heart" filter. He took a selfie. My dad TOOK A SELFIE ON SNAPCHAT. WHAT?!?!

When I got the notification on my phone, my first thought was, "Um, did he get hacked or has he gone crazy?!" My oh my, do I remember that day like it was yesterday. My iron man, my bestie, knew what would make me laugh and he gave it his all, never taking a moment for granted. Little moments like these let me know he was always thinking about me and I wasn't alone, no matter how alone I may feel.

To know that instead of experiencing that moment through Snapchat, I could've experienced it in person if I hadn't moved, still sends pangs of regret through my body. Through healing, I have learned to embrace the joy from that moment instead of focus on what could have been. That whole snapchat scene will forever make me laugh. The fact that my dad mustered the strength to scream out and send me a selfie just makes me giggle. We must forgive ourselves. We are not meant to carry that burden, rather, give it to God. He will be more than happy to carry it for you. Call out to Jesus, he is just a prayer away.

#GirlDad

Principle Four

THE HEALING
POWERS OF HOPE

Chapter 10

Speedy Hot Wheels

My dad wasn't just any dad, he was *my* dad. He became my identity after he was gone. The first thing in the morning, the last thought at night and everything in between, revolved around my "iron man" and I just couldn't see beyond my grief. Everything seemed to amplify his absence. The deep hole of depression began to fill with the even darker waters of anxiety. You know when you have a bad dream and you wake up and the relief that it was "just a dream" washes over you, then you return to your smiling, stretching, wonderful-morning self? Yeah, I couldn't wake up from my nightmare. No matter how many pinches I gave myself on the arm, this bad dream was my new reality.

My dad was my joy. He was my partner in crime. He

was my comedian. He was my doctor (he passed the medical board exams so for real he was my physician!). He was my everything.

Through this journey, one of the many lessons I've learned is that if it isn't aligned with any part of God's ultimate plan, then it just ain't happening. Due to his physical disability, my dad didn't get the opportunity to practice medicine at any hospital or clinic. My dad didn't let that hinder his love for medicine though. He continued to volunteer his time at research centers and wrote articles on the effects of hypnosis drugs. Look it up, Dr. Florendo Joya. #PROUDDAUGHTER moment. He had plans of retiring as a full-time doctor. He absolutely loved the medical field and having the ability to change and save lives. I remember when I started school for respiratory therapy, my dad was so excited that I was able to use *his* stethoscope. For my 6th grade science fair project, he taught me how to perform blood pressure screenings and record results. We monitored my dad's blood pressure and blood oxygenation every day, it was always so intriguing to him. His love for medicine and helping others was truly astonishing, but God had other plans.

"We plan the way we want to live, but only God makes us able to live it."

(PROVERBS 16:9 MSG)

Even though my dad wasn't clinically able to save lives, he did save many souls. His humor, loving kindness and courageous presence truly affected those around him. His walk of faith and actions to back it up, served as a leading example for others. I envision him walking through the gates of Heaven with a white doctor's coat, helping patients who are unconscious here on earth. Flying his plane from hospital to hospital, he always wanted to be a pilot, smiling as he blissfully navigates through the clouds. Who knows right? A girl can dream.

Whatever your career or life path—dentist, doctor, athlete, teacher, actor, coach, chef, model, wife, husband, janitor—you have God-given gifts to use. So, use them. Don't waste them. Every second you spend doing something you aren't meant to do is one second away from doing what you are *supposed* to do. If you tried placing me as dentist, I would be running around with floss in my hair trying to find some toothpaste; it would be a disaster. But if you put me on set with a script, I would own that scene. I tell people all the time, no matter what it is that you do for a job, from warehouse to White House, you have the God-given ability to positively influence those around you, if you so choose.

When I walked into a room for whatever modeling job or acting role I was auditioning for, my mom would remind me that I was not doing it for myself. Say what?!? But for real, I was doing it so that I could bring light and encouragement with God's love into any role I played. I was to always do my best in any job, as if I were doing it for God alone. I took that to heart and even got nicknamed as the "modeling chaplain."

When you lose someone, someone that held valuable space in your heart, you start spending so much, if not all, of your time trying to process what happened. I wish I could tell you that the sting of loss will fade away, like when people say "time heals all" but for me, time did not heal my wounds. Time revealed my wounds. God healed my wounds. Time buries the hurt, but God provides the hope.

You try so hard to remember your loved one, how they made you feel, how they looked, how they smelled. You try to move on, but you end up with tear stained pillows and a floor full of Kleenex. Maybe it sounds weird to you, but to this day, I still try to find the scent of my dad on his Bluetooth and eyeglasses (I know, I know, crazy right...grief causes you to do some bizarre things, lol). Imagining the sounds of my dad coming home, the ramp getting pulled out and dropping to the ground, the van door sliding, seeing our little "special" van, then "speedy hot wheels" zooming right into the house. Those memories. That's what I wanted to wake up to. I started reliving so much of the past that I got stuck there. I was forgetting the present, forgetting the moment and not looking forward to the future. I forgot what hope looked like and just focused on what I had instead of God's exciting plans for me. When you are filled with so much pain and hurt, you don't want to create any more memories without your special person, you just want to coast along. I cried oceans of tears those final two weeks that my dad was here. Right now, even as I am writing these words, there are tears rolling down my cheeks. I went to school for acting and they train you to cry on the spot. It was hard for me to cry that quick. Now, all I have to think about is my dad, and my eyes well up in seconds.

We, as a family, went to Yosemite a few weeks after my dad had passed. When I saw those tremendous, astonishing waterfalls, the only thing my mind associated it to were the tears I shed for my father. I wasn't a fun person to be around for a long time. Prior to his passing, I was known to be a fun, outgoing, super-extroverted soul, but that one year, I just...I just couldn't function in life. I couldn't live. I couldn't see. It was as if my vision was blurred. I literally had to pinch myself in order to *feel* something. I thank God every day that I didn't follow through with my emotions. God had me in his hands.

All we had was faith, unity, and a whole lot of laughter. My dad's love for his family spoke light years. I don't know anyone else who would choose to breathe through a straw to continue living, just so they could have more time with their family. My dad extended his life six more miraculous years in order to be with his family. Our identities were rooted in each other and God. You see my friend, your identity isn't based on your financial worth, health, status or career. None of that matters. What does matter, is what you do with what you were given. You need to get your eternal perspective goggles on and remember your true identity in Jesus; where your eternal home will be. Absorb God's truth and it will get you through the impossible in whatever career path or life crisis you're in. Use your God-given talents everywhere, not just for yourself, but for those around you. We are placed here on earth to love Jesus by loving others.

The enemy fights, puts in overtime, for those who have beautiful testimonies of life. Living to honor and glorify God. For those who have words of encouragement, shed light into darkness, and help others around them; those who have a relationship with God. The enemy will fight you on all fronts; using your mind to constantly replay the traumatic events of your life. He wants you stuck in bitterness and resentment. For me, my resentment started as soon as I woke up in the morning. A new day meant new pain in my dictionary. I didn't want to wake up to the reality of the new normal. I wanted to relive the good times, the good memories, before all of this suffering. I wanted things to return to the way they were before, endless happiness.

Happiness…something we take for granted over time. During my childhood and through college, my happiness was playing competitive soccer. I remember how my dad always came to the rescue. There was one game where I was so sick, I had started vomiting on the field. Here came "speedy hot wheels!" My dad sped out, high speed onto the soccer field. My dad was not able to walk, but he sure knew how to ride his wheelchair! He got right out into the middle of the field to yell at the referee. I think at one point his wheels got stuck in the grass…awkward. But he didn't care about awkwardness when it came to his family, all of that was thrown to the side. It was family over everything. Christy Wilson Beam, author of *Miracles from Heaven* said it perfectly, "there is no man stronger than the man who's willing to lay down his pride for his family." My dad put aside his pride from day one. Willing to do whatever it took to get better and healthier. No matter what, it was always God and family first in true iron man style.

Bring happiness to someone that you know needs it now. Everyone's happiness is different. Do something that you know would make them laugh and make sure those you love, feel your love. Make God and family high priorities in your life and you will sense the difference.

One thing that got us through the hard days, that made us resilient, was humor. People would be so amazed at how we were able to laugh during difficult times. They would always comment on our strength, but it wasn't really our strength, it was strength through God. We didn't have to preach to people about Jesus because they could see it in everything we did. We were simply living our lives grounded in God's love. People won't remember what you say, they'll remember what you do. And let me tell you something, my dad always *did*. He would do all kinds of things to demonstrate God's love and his love for us.

Dad traveled with me all over the states for my soccer tournaments. He would continually surprise me with sweet, little gestures. Like one time when he saw me struggling with my worn-out wallet, the next morning I walked down to the kitchen and low-and-behold, a brand-new wallet was sitting on the counter. Or on Valentine's Day one year, I was feeling lonely and in walks (well wheels) my dad with mochi ice cream and flowers. Every heartbreak I went through, he was there to listen and comfort me. Once a week my dad would text me the letter "K" (translation: that was him asking me if I was ok). He always wanted me to know that I was his princess and that he was there for me no matter where he was at the time. Funny random story, for my sweet sixteen party the theme was "Bling It Out" and my dad decided to wear, what seemed to be, a fifty-pound dog chain around his neck. I tried to sneak out of my own party to meet some friends and I kid you not, I saw fire bolts coming towards me from the kitchen, "speedy hot wheels" was not having it! There was no hiding from those high-speed wheels! Even little things that made me laugh showed how much he loved me. We would do cheek to cheek kisses and then sometimes, suddenly, he'd turn his head to kiss me instead. I would get annoyed while he laughed his butt off. I mean, I wasn't really annoyed but it was just fun to mess with each other. My mom would always joke and say that if my dad was able to walk, I probably wouldn't have any boyfriends. He was so protective over me, which made me love him even more. One night after I went off to college in Irvine, about two hours from my parent's house, I was at a dorm party and acting a little "too cool" for school. I wasn't responding to my dad's texts. My dad forced my mom to put him in the car and they drove all the way to my dorm… at two in the morning! When I finally responded, they were both relieved and turned back around to drive home. But I fully believe if I hadn't texted back, those speedy wheels would've been chillin' in the hallway of my dorm.

Writing about the good times gets me emotional. Reality hits with the realization that we will no longer have any more moments to laugh about. What I have in the brain bank is all I've got. But I think it's my dad who reminds me, that he doesn't have to be present in order to witness my life unfolding. He is always by my side, like a guardian angel, my angel. He's got the best seat in the house to watch God's ultimate plan be revealed. Everyday is a day closer to being reunited with my dad. He will forever be in my thoughts, always encouraging me to live my life to the fullest. The #GirlDad bond we had will never leave me. I am his voice now. What started out as a pinky promise on that fateful day is now a book, a book that tells his story. This book gives his pain a purpose.

A lot of close friends of my "iron man" dad came by during his final days and they were all reminiscing about the good times they shared. One story that made me smile was from the pastor at a local church that came to visit. This pastor had a doctor's appointment at the hospital where my dad was volunteering. He saw my dad from a distance, a white blur as he flew around at a crazy pace, "speedy hot wheels" not a second to waste...zoom, zoom, zoom! He never got paid for working at the hospital, but he used to sit in at numerous medical conferences with some of the top physicians, just to learn.

I was in my dad's room at the time of his death. When the physician looked me in the eyes after I kept begging for alternative solutions to keep him alive, and clearly said, "it's not about you." I will never forget that line spoken to me. It was the same phrase that Pastor Rick Warren used at the start of his book, *The Purpose Driven Life*, "It's not about you." It may sound harsh, but it's the truth. It's not about me. It's not about you. Pastor Rick Warren continues to say, "the purpose of your life is far greater than your own personal fulfillment, your peace of mind or even your happiness. It's far greater than your family, your career or even your wildest dreams and ambitions. If you want to know why you were placed on this planet, you must begin with God. You were born by his purpose and for his purpose." It's one of my all-time favorite books.

"What is life?" His favorite CNA, Heather, told me that's the line my dad would often say while she was feeding him. Heather always treated and cared for my dad like he was her own. Our family felt comfortable knowing it was her shift on duty. Heather not only cared for him at the nursing home, but she came to the hospital to care for him one last time. She told us how cute he was whenever he would smirk. We will always and forever be thankful for that girl. Other staff members came to visit and a handful of them also treated my dad with special care.

Whenever I came to hang out with my dad, I always wanted to be outside or in the lobby. Sitting outside in front of my dad's nursing facility was a treat for us because he rarely was able to go outdoors. We would sit and talk about some of the new opportunities I was handed, he would aptly listen with his big 'ol eyes. He made me feel like everything I said was vitally important with his exaggerated expressions. We would walk across the street to this hotel lobby, one of our main spots to just chill and people watch. He'd get so upset every time I'd eat the complimentary hotel food and coffee. My dad, in his speedy hot wheels, would go around bragging to everyone about his daughter. He would always point to the TV whenever I was on and tell everyone around, "that's my daughter!" Now, I get to point to Heaven, saying, "that's my dad."

The manager at the nursing facility e-mailed my mom saying how much my dad will be missed, always scooting around and boasting about his wonderful family. He was a proud father. If you're a dad reading this right now, from a daughter's perspective, hearing that your father spoke highly of you all the time is something we cherish dearly. Don't have any shame with your pride. Be their biggest fans. #GirlDad

All those times my dad would guilt trip me whenever I was about to leave, was his way of telling me how much he valued his treasure. He always wanted to protect me from the world and keep me safe. Looking back, there were so many moments I wish I could have done more. More time, more photos, more kisses, more posts, more phone calls, more everything. You don't realize what you have until it's gone. As cliché as that saying is, it's true. Just to see him look at himself in the mirror again, not out of vanity, but to make sure he didn't still have his dinner on his chin, ha, just to see him smile once more... what I would give.

We had such a unique, fun #GirlDad relationship. I remember how funny my dad was. He was a comedian. He never allowed his disability to hinder his love and humor for his family. When he laughed hard, his nose would scrunch up in such a way that caused you to laugh yourself. There are so many memories with Mr. Speedy Hot Wheels, too many to list. But if there's anything I can take away or hope that you, as a reader can take away, it's that we must live our best lives.

LIVE LIFE, my friend. I say it a lot in this book, but I mean it...LIVE, LAUGH, LOVE. ALWAYS.

Friend, you are special, unique, and created in the image of Jesus. So go, waste no time in pursuing your gifts, embracing hope, speeding your way right over the small stresses in life. Give your worries to God and live out your purpose. Aspire to Inspire.

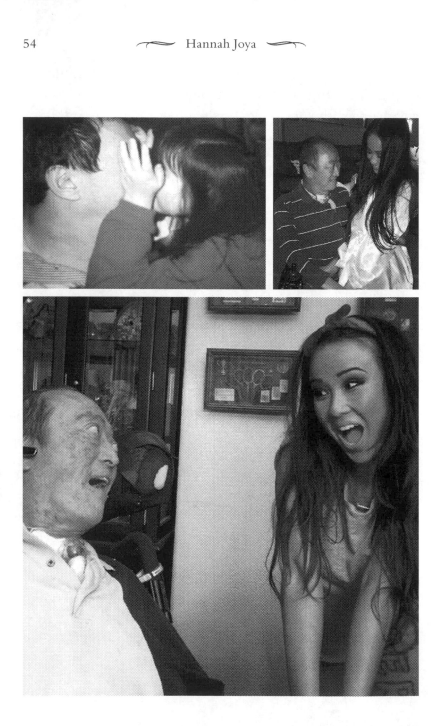

Chapter 11

Love & Laughter

"The only thing that counts is faith expressing itself through love."

(GALATIANS 5:6 NIV)

"Take my kidney!" I cried, volunteering myself to be a candidate as my dad's kidney donor. I'll never forget the response from the doctors, "there is nothing else we can do, his body has completely shut down." What do you mean there's nothing else you can do? There is ALWAYS something that can be done. My dad ALWAYS got out of the impossible. What made this time different? There must be a mistake, run some more tests. Not a big deal. He's just tired. He needs sleep. Give him some time to recuperate—the denial was real for me. "Your dad will not be leaving this room," spoken again to me, by another doctor. This is pure insanity. My dad always got out of every hospital. We knew as a family there was going to come a time when my dad's body would become resistant to any antibiotics given, we knew that, we just weren't ready. I mean, how can you ever *really* prepare for something like this? No one is every *really* ready for death. My dad had both lungs filled with fluid one time, the worst case of pneumonia possible, and he miraculously healed from that. Why is this time any different? I don't understand. This was the biggest hit. The toxicity reports came back and it was in his blood. His body was done fighting and we knew that. His body was telling us that he was ready, even if he couldn't tell us. I remember standing over his bed begging him to wake up. I felt as If my dad's new spiritual presence was beside me, standing strong, comforting me, wiping away my tears. I tried to ignore those feelings because I wanted him to be physically present, not just spiritually.

That day was when I learned to surrender. You see that's the beauty about love. When you love someone, you're willing to sacrifice yourself for that person, even if it's just a part of yourself, like a kidney. I never knew I had the ability to cry so much until that day. I even developed a wrinkle between my eyebrows (heavy moisture and HydraFacial's to the rescue!).

There is a popular San Diego beach down the street from the hospital. I went there every day that week, sat in my car, and just started screaming. Yelling until I couldn't yell anymore. Going ballistic, ape crazy. Imagine the people in the cars next to me trying to enjoy the sunset…sorry strangers.

God calls us to be real with Him. For me being real was being angry and bitter, my heart had become callus. My dad sacrificed his life to just be there because he loved us. He gave us six more years of his life by breathing through a tracheostomy cannula, which is said to be like breathing through a straw. He would rather suffer everyday than to lose precious time with his family. That's the type of character my dad had, #GirlDad.

My friend, sacrifice is essential when you love someone. Being willing to sacrifice is not easy. It may not come down to you having to breathe through a straw, but think about how you are blessed. You are blessed with lungs to breathe. So, breathe. Tell your loved ones how much they mean to you every chance you get. Reflect on your life and how God has directed, guided and provided.

With that being said, of course, I have another story to tell you about a special memory with my dad. One nursing facility we were at hosted a Halloween party every year for the residents and their families. Then there was my dad, Mr. Too-Cool-For-School (hmmmm, that must be where I got it from…) who hated attending these events. Now, I loved them, and had decided to dress up as a bumble bee. My dad was in a sad mood that morning so I searched for something he could wear to participate in the party. Low and behold I found a red bandana. I quickly wrapped it around my dad's head without his consent, grabbed my phone, had someone take our picture, then immediately posted it on Instagram. I captioned it, "stick close to your thuggish honey and BEE a thug." My dad didn't get it. I don't get it either, if we're really being honest here. But it sounded fitting enough for the GRAM! Like they say, if you don't post it, did it really happen?

At some point, we'll all wake up on the wrong side of the bed. I definitely don't wake up every day feeling like a breath of fresh air and sunshine with rainbows. There are going to be tough days. But you see my friend, it doesn't really matter how you get someone to laugh, even if it makes absolutely no sense at all, it just matters that they laugh. There's no surprise as to why there are "yoga laughter classes" because laughter is proven to increase happiness. Make the most of any situation that life hands you. When life throws you lemons…don't just make lemonade…add some extra, organic honey, kick back, and just "bee" happy (see what I did there, wink, wink).

Here's to the beauty and freedom of choice. We are not robots; we are given the option to choose. Throughout all those days that my dad was sick in the hospital, our family chose humor. We chose laughter. We chose love. We chose to bring everyone together to enjoy life for what it was. Beauty and joy can be found in even the simplest of things. Our family was and still is, blessed. And because we are so blessed, we *choose* to bless others. I have so many precious memories to this day because I chose LIFE.

Today, right now, you have the freedom to choose what kind of life you want to live. I hope you choose love and laughter; you won't be disappointed.

"A cheerful heart is good medicine, but a crushed spirit dries up the bones."

(PROVERBS 17:22 NIV)

Chapter 12

Waves of Grief

"Papa is flying with a big smile in the sky" my youngest nephew, Gabe responded after seeing pictures of my dad. Like wait! What? A three-year-old speaking like that. I asked again, thinking maybe he drank too much milk or something. Instantly, he pointed to the sky and started making a hand-flying motion, almost like a butterfly. He then pointed to his mouth, showing us a big smile. Gabe was too young to really remember my dad, but he seemed to know exactly who was in that photo and was adamant about it. I wholeheartedly believe that my nephew saw my dad as like an angel. Kids see things that the rest of us miss; they have a pure special connection to the world around them that we somehow grow out of as we age.

My dad isn't here physically, but I can tell you that I feel his presence everywhere I go. When you love someone so much and they pass from this world to the next life, I believe we are gifted with a forever guardian angel; always in our hearts. The son of a well-known Christian music artist, TobyMac, unexpectedly lost his son and released the song, "21 years" in dedication to his son's memory. A line from his song hits home for me, "Are you singing with the angels? Are you happy where you are? Well until this show is over, and you run into my arms, God has you in Heaven, but I have you in my heart." I know he is singing with the angels as I sing along in praise or sing along to this song. He never leaves my heart or my mind. And that's the funny thing, or I guess not so funny thing about grief. One moment you feel one way and the next your ugly crying. Sometimes the smallest of things will bring the biggest of waves.

I've been to plenty of funerals throughout my life where people have lost loved ones who didn't have Jesus. The grief and hurt they endure come with so much more confusion and hopelessness. I've been to celebrations of life as well, you reminisce, you try to stay positive, but it still doesn't take away their absence, which is ironic because how can you take away something that isn't there. Grief is simply love unspoken; it's the love you are no longer able to give to a person because they are physically gone. I took comfort in knowing that my dad is in a better place, that even though he is gone, he is pain free and can still receive the love I have to give in his own special way. We can take comfort in the hope that it's never really goodbye. That's the reason I chose the title of this book. I may not see him soon, or at least I hope not because God still has further purpose in my life, but I know that I will see him eventually. Knowing the truth, knowing that one day I will be in paradise, has completely shifted my perspective. We will call it my "earthly perspective," but whatever you want to call it, the way I had been looking at life was preventing me from seeing the beauty of it. My thoughts began to shift, my curiosity drove me forward into what I would call a "godly perspective" and I began to see more of a purpose; achieving my life's mission, whatever God deems that to be.

That shift took time and patience. Grief is a process and working through grief is never easy. For me, it was too unbearably painful to know I would never see my dad again. My iron man, my dad, transitioned into his new life on June 13, 2018. It was only four days until Father's Day. As if that wasn't already bad enough, my dad's birthday was only four days after Father's Day. The realization was like a ton of bricks smacking me in the face. I felt as if the world was against me. I became voiceless. Emotionless. A lost cause. I wouldn't get out of bed and I would just stare, wide-eyed, at the ceiling until nightfall, with a blanket of used tissues covering my head. All it took was one scroll down social media, seeing all the "HAPPY FATHER'S DAY!" posts before I spiraled back down into my grief grave. I'm not trying to be dramatic, I truly felt dead to the world. The reality of his death would just keep hitting me over and over again until I simply couldn't get up from my bed.

When the spoken and written condolences dwindle down, when the visitors stop visiting, the "Are you okay?" text messages become fewer and farther between, the baskets of food at the front door stop appearing—that is when you begin to experience the genuine sadness for what you've lost. That, my friends, is grief. And grief doesn't just sit at your door, it incessantly rings the doorbell. It knocks and knocks until you want to pull out your hair and scream. It's something I wish I didn't have to start learning at such a young age. I had a psychologist tell me once that my whole life had been a life ridden with grief. With every sickness my dad had, with the frequent thoughts, "Could this be his last day here on earth?" with each and every pain that became our pain, it was grief. The day I felt grief in its truest form was the day my dad left this earth.

Grief is hard. Grief is ugly. Honestly, I really don't like that word, grief. The word grief even sounds unappealing to me. I wasn't ready to hear the word let alone begin the grief process. I was never going to have my future children say, "Grandpa" or have him zoom them around on his electric wheelchair. The image of my dad in his electric wheelchair guiding me down the aisle at my wedding then accidentally runnning over my dress as we laugh, it wasn't going to happen. My future husband wouldn't be able to ask for my hand in marriage. We all wouldn't be together for birthdays or milestones. There was so much to life that I had yet to experience with my dad. Dreams that would never come to fruition. He was sixty-three years old and I was twenty seven, that's just not enough time. Often times I prayed that God would just take me instead.

My dad had been telling us he for a while that he was ready to go home to Heaven. I just wasn't ready to accept that. I didn't want to even hear it. I saw my dad, truly, as my superhero, my IRON MAN.

I brought balloons to my dad's hospital room like I usually did on his birthday that final week. I told the doctors that when my dad wakes up, he would see that it was his sixty-fifth birthday (I was so delusional, he was actually turning sixty-four, I got the wrong number of balloons). They put their heads down. I knew what that meant without them even telling me. Grief causes you to do things that don't match up with reality. Your mind is somewhere else.

When his body was shutting down and going into complete toxic shock, slipping into a coma, he was no longer able to urinate. I became desperate. I even promised that I wouldn't go to the bathroom until he did. I drove home that night and passed out on the kitchen floor right in front of my mom. I couldn't handle, couldn't grasp what was happening and my mind was spinning. I couldn't handle my dad being in the state he was. I went to CVS the next day and bought those warm, hand pouch things to help stimulate urination. That didn't work. I tried ancient oils that we had from Israel, that didn't work either. Nothing was working. I even researched magicians to come "heal" him, I honestly don't even know what I was thinking, I had reached a level of desperation I had never experienced before. I couldn't accept what was happening. I drove to the beach down the street every day that week to scream and yell at God. I cursed him. Anger and hatred fueled my tantrums, I had so much rage in my heart towards God. I threw my bible across my room every night. I wasn't okay.

My mind was not mentally grasping everything that was happening. It took me up until the actual day of my dad's passing for me to accept the inevitable. I wanted to fight for my dad until the end because I knew he would have done the exact same for me. I felt as if I had become his advocate, his voice and I was going to be heard. I begged the doctors to take my kidney for him; we all knew that wouldn't even be possible.

The days immediately following my dad's passing were a blur. My sweet family took us to Yosemite to be submerged in its breath-taking natural beauty. Even then, my grief was preventing me from seeing the beauty in nature, I couldn't see the beauty in anything at that point. I was still in shock. I couldn't bring myself to eat and because of that, I lost 20 pounds.

Here's the thing about grief: it comes in unexpected waves. I had heard that before, but I never understood what it meant until I had to go through it myself. People were saying to me, "I can't even imagine what it's like losing a dad." Well, to be honest I couldn't imagine either, but I didn't have a choice. You really don't know how strong you are until being strong is the only option.

When someone you know is dealing with grief, whatever the loss may be, please be the first to reach out to them with an open mind. Even if you don't know what to say, just gently reach out with a loving heart and offer to help; to listen or just be present. Let them know you're thinking about them and ask them how they're doing. Many have said, "Oh, no, give them space, give them time to be alone" but I couldn't imagine being alone. Alone!? Though that may be healthy and needed for some people, for me, I needed the opposite. Being alone everyday caused me to fall into a deep depression. It allowed my thoughts to turn into anxiety. I can't even begin to tell you how much it meant when someone would text me, asking me how I was doing or asking if I needed anything. A girlfriend texted me daily after my dad passed. She would always end the text by saying, "Don't feel the need to text back, just know I'm here." Often, when we're experiencing grief, we become numb, alone and insecure. The new normal feels so abnormal. We don't know what to do. We become withdrawn and fade away into the crevices of our bed. Living the new normal just doesn't feel right.

That person may respond with an "I'm fine" or "I'm ok" or "I'm just taking things day by day," and most likely they aren't "fine" but being acknowledged, letting them know they aren't forgotten, may just save a life. When I would get messages, to me it meant that I was loved, that someone actually cared enough to contact me. It was when the messages stopped that I felt lonely again, the weight of reality rushing back at me full force. Yes, I know...I shouldn't be putting my happiness in another persons' hands, only true fulfillment can come from God. I know, I know. But hey…I'm only human. At that time, it was comforting. I would get a message, begin to feel somewhat ok and reassured, ready to start the day and then BOOM! I'd be hit with the realization that no message was ever going to bring my dad back and the grief cycle would start all over again. It was a constant battle; it was as if sadness had become an addiction.

Please be gentle with those who are grieving. It was hard to swallow words from those who would tell me I would get over it within a certain time frame or to just move on and keep busy. When people asked my mom if she was starting to date, that was hard for me to hear without getting angry. Please be kind with your words. Offer an ear to listen, a cup for coffee, a lunch date; it's the sweet, small gestures that help those in pain. The ones who brought me random matcha lattes, who simply showed up even when I didn't ask for it, that's what brought me comfort. Asking for help is hard enough, but couple that with grief and it just becomes another task. I had a good friend bring me clothes because I had no strength to even change my outfit. I couldn't listen to music or noise because all I wanted to hear was my dad's voice. I would call my dad's phone just to see his name on my call log. I'd overplay all the videos we took together just to see him smile again, anything to subdue the heart wrenching replay of those last seconds he had on earth. I tried erasing it from my memory, but I couldn't. Every sound was a trigger. Every time I would hear someone breathe it would be a trigger. Every time I saw a wheelchair it would trigger me. Everything seemed like a trigger. I was drowning in this trigger ridden world of PTSD moments and couldn't catch my breath from the intolerable, painful thoughts.

Everyone grieves differently and there's no right or wrong

manual on "How to Grieve" so take your time, allow the emotions to flow and be compassionate towards yourself. <u>In order to heal, you must be real.</u> You're not healing on anyone else's timetable.

God answers your prayers in special ways. You're not alone, my friend. Feel the rush of comfort during your time of hopelessness. Healing is around the corner. You don't have to grieve alone; God weeps with you. Allow His healing hands to bring you back to life.

> *"The LORD is close to the brokenhearted and saves those who are crushed in spirit."*
>
> (PSALM 34:18 NIV)

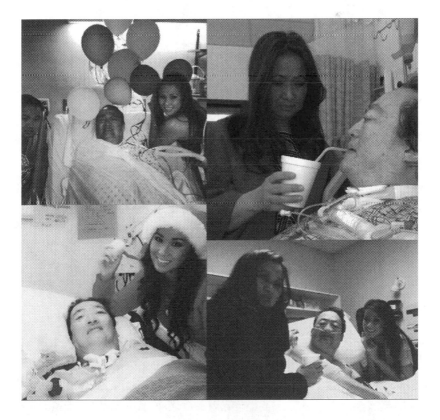

Chapter 13

Hurt People will Hurt People

I know what it feels like to not receive love. To not be pursued. To feel worthless. To feel that everyone else is so perfectly happy in their fairytale relationships. Heartaches aren't given a painful name for nothing. Here is the thing about people who are hurting, they too will hurt others because misery loves company.

Break-ups are the worst. I mean there are obviously worse things, hence the book about losing my father, but break-ups are still horrible. And when you have a void and you try to fill it with things in order to numb the reality you're living in; it never ends well. The enemy knows your weakness; he knows where your heart longs to be. He is like a snake, slithering through tall grass, waiting and watching for just the right moment to attack. And at your weakest moment, your breaking point, that's when he comes to kill and destroy.

My weakness was finding companionship for all the wrong reasons in all the wrong ways and in all the wrong places. Due to my dad's disability, I didn't receive the type of physical love I was constantly craving in order to feel secure. I was never the type of girl who just dated around. When I was in committed relationships, I was already planning my wedding; where the ceremony would be held, who my bridesmaids would be, what type of food we'd have. I was on *that* level when it came to commitment. I was raised by parents who taught me that sex was only to be used within marriage and not before. No living together until marriage. No drinking. No sleepovers. That's the type of foundation, the type of morals I was raised on. So, breakups to me were as if we were getting divorced. It was like the end of the world and we were going to have to figure out who would get custody of my heart. I was so eager to be loved, so hungry for it that I began to look in the wrong places and compromise my morals. I knew I wanted to be with someone who had a solid relationship with Jesus, but I had begun to make exceptions and when souls don't have Jesus, they don't know how to love properly.

<u>God is love</u>; He is not the best source of love, He *is* love. If someone doesn't have God in their life then how can they possibly know love? We humans can only imitate God's love and the further away we drift from Him, the less we know of love; it becomes a faint shadow of what real love is.

Much of my life that was spent in ICU waiting rooms and nursing homes was not just spent dealing with the anxiety about my dad's health, but also the anxiety that goes with infidelity. There were numerous instances of unfaithfulness in my previous relationships, the repercussions from that have taken me years to overcome. The toxicity from those relationships seeped into my very core, causing me to lose my identity; I had to rediscover who I was over the years. Insecurity seemed to be my motto. I couldn't understand my worth, my self-esteem was shot and I was broken. If I couldn't love myself, how would I be able to love others? If I only knew and believed in God's love for me at the time; I was already enough. I didn't have to chase his love, I didn't have to prove my worth, I was already seen and accepted by Jesus. Our first, true love.

It's insane how a broken persons' insecurities can transfer to an innocent participant in the relationship. How they can warp your mind into thinking that you aren't good enough and you're the reason the cheating happened in the first place. Constant thoughts like, "Only if I were prettier, skinnier or more accomplished then maybe he wouldn't want someone else" or thinking that "I was always nagging, so it's my fault," please realize, it's NOT you! God calls us to forgive, but he doesn't call us to allow others to harm us, mentally, spiritually or physically. I wish my mom's wisdom on this hadn't fallen on deaf ears. I wish I had listened to her when she spoke this truth onto me, but my judgement was clouded at the time. Listen to your loved ones, they have your best interest at heart.

It was hard to find a place to start over again after a major heartache or being cheated on. When others would inform me about the cheating, it just caused me to dislike other women and become jealous, and ain't nobody got time for that! This is exactly what our enemy wants. The enemy wants you to be done, destroyed, discouraged and doubting. He wants you to envy and compare. He wants distortion and confusion. The sad truth is, the enemy will use people to hurt you; many times, that person has no idea they are being used. Pray that God will not let you be used to hurt someone else or that you will have the discernment to know the difference.

I know that hopeless feeling of starting from the ground up. You don't even want to go out to restaurants by yourself or with friends because you've lost your sense of independence. I told myself countless times that "this will be the last time" and that "I'll forgive," but when is it really going to be the last time my friend? The last time being verbally abused. The last time being physically abused. The last time your spirit is torn apart.

> *"Be kind and compassionate to one another, forgiving*
> *each other, just as in Christ God forgave you."*
> (EPHESIANS 4:32 NIV)

Is it possible to forgive? Yes. Yes, it is. Forgiveness is letting go even if the person who hurt you has no remorse. Forgiving takes strength. I know what it's like to forgive those who don't care to apologize, but forgiving wasn't just for them, it was for me. I was battling grief over my father as well as the grief that comes with broken relationship, after broken relationship; one after another. We live in a very broken world filled with hurt, heart breaks and heart aches are inevitable. My sweet friend, find your value in Jesus. Forgive those who hurt you not so they can be off the hook but so you can free yourself from that unnecessary bondage. When you depend on anyone else besides Jesus to give you love and comfort, it will eventually fail. In the end, it was far worse for me to grieve two losses because I was constantly seeking to fill a void with empty relationships. In my desperation I failed to see God who was so desperately waiting for me.

I would have all the facts. I had people calling me, texting me, providing me with all the evidence I needed to confirm the unfaithful acts happening behind my back. I promise you this, girls can be the best "FBI agents" for real, but despite the accurate conviction, in the end it comes down to this one simple thing: I would demand the respect I thought I deserved. And if I didn't know my worth, there was no way I could truly understand the level of respect I deserved.

I was committed to being broken, to tolerating unfaithfulness, disloyal, damaged relationships. I essentially committed myself to the kind of love that left an identity shattered. The kind that woke me up at 3am with heavy, gut-wrenching anxiety. The kind that forced me to buy waterproof mascara from all the tears shed. Each time I compromised my worth, it stole a piece of me; it stole a part of me that I needed for grieving my father. It distracted me from truly processing all the emotions that came with my dad's disability. It clouded my mind with lies as I attempted to unravel the confusion that coincides with infidelity in relationships. My concentration, once again, was blurred with fog; drowned in depression.

I had to make the decision, by the grace of God, to know what my worth and value was. I had to decide if I was going to listen to what someone said I was or who God said I was. According to God, we are all (that includes you) worthy of being loved and pursued. There were times I was the one pursuing; chasing down love like it was the last roll of toilet paper in Walmart. I had a bright, pink neon sign on my head that screamed "desperate." That's not love my friend. That's insecurity. That's not knowing who you are, what you stand for and who you belong to. You are the daughter and son of a king clothed in royal jewels. Believe that. Walk that. Do not make time for broken souls who don't know your worth or understand your value like God does. Sweet friend, you are a diamond! Shine bright in this broken world. Settle for nothing less than the best. You are the daughter, son, child of a ROYAL KING. And don't you ever forget it.

Turn your attention to seeking God rather than people. That's when the healing begins, including the breaking of mental abuse, physical abuse and sexual ties. No longer will you be held captive. No longer slaves to the hurt and the pain. God's love will anchor you down.

It wasn't an overnight prayer. It took years. How many times a day did I have to repeat out loud, "I am worthy and valuable" UNTIL I ACTUALLY BELIEVED IT. I'm so beyond thankful for all the broken people that didn't know how to love. Now, I understand through God's love that if it hadn't been for them, I wouldn't know how to forgive the unforgivable. I wouldn't know what it was like to be treated well, if I hadn't been treated so wrong. I learned that hope for the future and hope for putting the pieces back together started with painful forgiveness. But no pain goes unnoticed and, in the end, pain creates resilience. Use your pain to fuel your strength. You are stronger than you know.

#GirlDad

Principle Five

RENEWING RESILIENCE

Chapter 14

Lobby Love

I believe that we all have "lobbies" within our soul. It is how we greet people with our open hearts and meet them with compassion.

When my dad was able to escape his ventilator machine for a few hours, he would head down to the lobby of the nursing facility and spend those two hours greeting everyone that entered. Most of those that crossed the threshold did so with anxiety, worry, sadness, and despair; dreading whatever news was about to come their way regarding their loved one's debilitating state. Morning, afternoon or night, you could count on seeing my dad right there in the lobby greeting people with his smile. Even though he was no longer able to practice medicine, he was still saving lives through love.

Loving people with a simple smile. Smiles can save someone. I truly believe they can bring miracles; a smile delivered at just the right time could mean the world to someone. Many of these resident family members and friends would come up to us and tell us how meaningful it was to be greeted by my dad. They would divulge how that simple smile compelled them to reflect on the reality of life. Here is a man who is clearly paralyzed with a spirit more alive than most of us in our best of days. A spirit that could never be squashed and a spirit that is spread through a smile.

No matter where our lives take us, whether it's a hospital, a nursing facility or the luxury of our own home, we are in charge of creating our very own *lobby*. God is ever present, greeting those who we allow to enter our sacred space. It is always our choice to open our hearts to strangers, provide a smile to anyone who glances our way, and welcome people with open arms. You never know when your choice will be the difference between someone's good or bad day. Your choice has a trickle effect that does not just touch one life, but anyone else that person may encounter.

When my dad was still living at home, he would sit outside and became known in our community as the "security guard." Our neighbors would feel safer having dad out there on standby, greeting people and waving. He would be in his electric wheelchair, sometimes completely leaned back in a sleeping position, basking in the sunshine, which inevitably led to what looked like an "orange peel" spray tan. There were times I would come home after school to find my dad sleeping with his 3lb chihuahua, Coco, perched on his lap. I'd honk the horn, scaring the skittles out of him; he probably would have jumped right out of his chair if his body would've let him.

We'd all laugh, and my mom would say I was the spice of his life. I was constantly keeping him on his toes and causing his heart to skip a beat, in a good way of course, wink, wink. Who wants to live a boring life!?

See, my friend, no matter where we are in life, God calls us to love and smile and laugh.

My dad was considered to be the sickest of the sick patients wherever we went. No cure. Nothing that would help him be able to walk again. We were just putting bandaids over gaping wounds everywhere we went. But that didn't stop my dad from trying every type of treatment out there. Even up until the last week before he passed, he still made appointments for his infusions. Yes, my dad was tired and often said he was ready to go see his creator; I mean who wouldn't. The amount of pain and the length of time he had to endure that pain; I mean how much can one endure? My dad was so paralyzed that even the smallest of movements took an immense amount of energy and strength. If you were to see photos of him over the years, you would see cuts and bruises all over his arms from the daily injections he received. Imagine getting shots everyday...yeah, no. It was oftentimes a struggle to find a vein on my dad which meant not getting poked once but over and over again. He would feel every poke.

I went to urgent care last week from a stomach pain I was feeling. What was supposed to be a two-hour visit turned into an eight-hour visit. As I was lying there, I imagined my dad. I was getting so restless, wanting to go home. Hurting from all the needle pokes. Thinking about how my dad had twenty-seven years of that. He was never giving up, no matter how much he went through. His heart was made of passion, his fight made of iron, and his soul made of love. That's where I realized he truly was "Iron Man" and there was no other name more suitable for him.

To this day, when I go to the clinic to get my regular

checkups, I walk through many of the spots where I vividly remember my dad and his smile. I smile now, knowing that he's no longer pinned down to his wheelchair. He no longer has to withstand hours of medicinal infusions. He's now running the streets of gold, smiling still.

What's putting you down in life? What's holding you back or pinning you down? What's paralyzing you with fear? Greeting people, allowing people to feel seen and loved is what we're here to do. That's our purpose: to love. We love because HE first loved us.

Create a space, mentally, that becomes your "lobby" and in this area ready yourself to invite broken souls craving to be loved. Simply smile at the souls you see because in reality, we are all broken and hurting. We are all running in the human race together so let's not compete but rather compliment.

Sad backwards is "das" and das not good! Ha, smile! Laugh! Let's get weird in our self-made lobbies together! We aren't meant to be alone. The world needs more loving lobbies, so let's show them our ornate foyers, show them our sparkling chandeliers, and our grand staircases that lead to infinite possibilities.

> *"Love is patient, love is kind. It does not envy, it does not boast, it is not proud. It does not dishonor others, it is not self-seeking, it is not easily angered, it keeps no record of wrongs. Love does not delight in evil but rejoices with the truth. It always protects, always trusts, always hopes, always perseveres. Love never fails. But where there are prophecies, they will cease; where there are tongues, they will be stilled; where there is knowledge, it will pass away."*
>
> (1 CORINTHIANS 13:4-8 NIV)

Chapter 15

"Selfie"

O ne thing my dad and I had in common was our love for taking pictures. Everywhere we went, I would look around to find the closest person to snap a photo. My dad would straighten up, cross his arms over his chest, lookin' like a boss, truly confident with his princess by his side, and a smile so wide…after he passed, these were the photos I cherished. All I had after twenty-seven years of life was memories through photos.

Sometimes we have so many memories, so many events, that we simply can't remember them all which is why we take these beautiful snapshots of life. To remind us of the big and the little moments.

I created a Facebook page for him during our journey and my sister-in-law, Grace, created a blog in order to document our time together. Grace talked about the days where it was necessary for my dad to use a straw in his mouth and point at letters in the alphabet in order to communicate his wants and needs. She also talked about the time when my parents created their own version of a morse code system whenever they were talking to each other over the phone. My mom would call and ask him if he was ok, since he couldn't speak, he would respond with clicking noises. If he responded with two tongue clicks, that meant he was ok and if he made A LOT of clicking noises that meant that she needed to come to the hospital immediately. Later on, in this book you will get to see the actual blogs from Grace, so you too can put yourself in our little and big life moments. It's so interesting to go back and see the exact details, remembering the specifics within each moment. You are in for a treat my friend.

We all found ways to exclusively communicate with my dad, for me, it was with photos. We loved taking selfies; using all the filters on Snapchat and then having a deep, belly laugh session together afterwards. We would often take ten photos in the same pose or with the same filter just because I think he loved the process, loved smiling, and loved sharing this moment with his princess.

Dads have such a vital role in their daughters' lives. Dads can have many jobs in their life, but the one job that takes precedence above all else is actually *being a dad* to his daughter. Or at least it's my belief that it should be. Not everyone can be as lucky as me. To have a dad who was truly, without a doubt, one hundred percent committed, to being the best dad to his daughter. And that's exactly what he was…*the best* dad.

He was always thoughtful, too. On my birthday, he would

make sure that the dozen roses he ordered were delivered before I got there, so that when I walked in, they were the first thing I would see. On Mother's Day, he had the nursing staff write my mom a letter on his behalf and pestered her until she opened the laptop, pleasantly surprised by his heartfelt sentiments. He also loved bonding with my brother whether it was shopping at electronic stores or stopping at a hot dog stand. The simple things in life can often times be the most unforgettable.

There were so many times my family would say "no more pictures!" and I'm so glad I never listened and took 500. Those photos remind us all of the love we shared; I need that reminder now more than ever. Take as many photos as you can. Take a selfie and send it to someone who needs a smile. Let them know you're thinking of them. Appreciate those you love, hug them a little tighter, forgive quicker and laugh longer. Cherish each moment, in the moment, and make sure you have photos that can take you back to those specific moments in time. You won't regret it my friend.

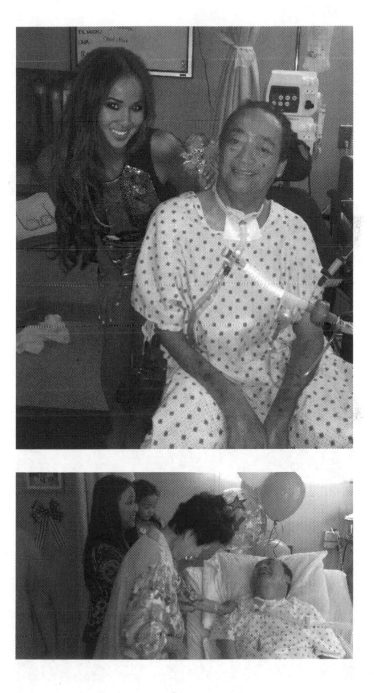

My dad no matter how sick he got, was always saying "im doing good"..and giving the glory an praise to God, every single day

#GirlDad

Principle Six

LEARNING TO TRUST
IN HIM VS. EMOTIONS

Chapter 16

10,000 Reasons

"And on that day
When my strength is failing
The end draws near
And my time has come
Still my soul will
Sing your praise unending
Ten thousand years
And then forevermore"
–Matt Redman (10,000 Reasons, Bless the Lord)

The week that he passed was when I first noticed he was responding differently to treatments. Since he was a doctor, my dad had always been so demanding of the nurses as he knew exactly what should be done. On one particular day he told them he didn't want to get any more pokes from injections, and he was done getting his blood drawn. I thought he was giving up at the time. I got so upset when I heard that and I told him, "Man up and get that shot if you want to live." We used tough love a lot with my dad and that's how he managed to get through most of the painful moments. However, this time my iron man, my best friend was not giving up, he was just giving it to God. What painful moments are you holding on to? What stresses are you burdened with? What are your reasons for not letting it go or letting it control your life? Give it to God, allow Him to help you heal.

My dad had a life before paralysis. Before being diagnosed with GBS/CIDP disease. Before he became a husband, a dad and a grandpa. Before it all, my dad was a son and a brother. He was a mama's boy and he was good to everyone around him. He was a licensed physician who passed what was considered to be one of the hardest board exams within the medical field. Following all the rejection letters that came from different hospitals (during the early stages of his disability), he continued attending a community college, wanting to learn more. He worked hard and studied harder. My dad had so much confidence when he was wheeling himself around to classes, asking people to open the doors for him, not skipping a single beat on his learning path. He should have won an award for perseverance. He actually did win quite a few awards for courageous acts. One of the awards he received was in 2015 at the GBS/CIDP Foundation Fashion show. I got to model down the runway as well as present my dad with the "Robert and Estelle Benson

Award" for resilience; he was the first ever recipient. My hero and I also had the opportunity to speak in front of 500 managers for a large health organization conference regarding my dad's story, where he was honored with a standing ovation. He always found a reason to keep going.

Dr. Florendo Joya receiving his award: and he is the very first recipient of the Robert and Estelle Benson Award for the San Diego chapter, And Dr. Joya is known as "The Man Who Never Stops Fighting"

My dad was involved in my life far more than I could have ever imagined. For birthdays, he made picture slide shows with all these cheesy graphics for my friends and I to watch, each slide show taking almost a year to create. He would also get dressed up for my birthday theme parties. He was there for every graduation, every soccer game, every audition, every photoshoot; no matter what city or location, my dad was there. He would even show up at sleepovers to make sure I was safe… parked in a van with my mom down the street like stalkers, ha, total Dad move. But he always found a reason to be there.

My dad handled rejections every day. EVERYDAY. Morning to night. He had twenty-seven years of pure rejection. He replaced every rejection with redirection. He knew the direction he was heading; it wasn't his plan; it was God's plan. Do you know how many times we could have filed reports for all the wrongdoings toward my dad? There was so much unnecessary suffering, so many dehumanizing incidents, so much injustice. And he wasn't the only one, but he was the only person who I witnessed it with day in and day out. I got into countless arguments with employees who were treating my father but not treating him with respect; not treating him as the competent, well educated, and mentally sound person that he was. I was constantly trying to protect him from people who only saw him as a number, which often led to my mother being embarrassed *a lot*. We would pray before care meetings; we would pray that the staff would see our father the way we saw him. Even though my dad could hold his own, I felt the need to be his advocate. It makes me think about all the other people who don't have advocates. We need to see people for who they are…***people!*** Treating everyone as if they were your loved one, seeing them with fresh eyes, exhibiting compassion, demonstrating love with every action; having patience for patients. If only everyone could view the world from another's perspective when they encounter them, how different our world would be.

"Above all, love each other deeply, because love covers over a multitude of sins."

(1 PETER 4:8 NIV)

This world is a broken place filled with injustice, indescribable pain, and a multitude of sorrows. If we had not been there for my dad every day, if we weren't his reasons, he would have lost hope, lost his purpose, and in turn lost his life, a long time ago. There are hundreds of patients who don't have family members to support and love them, let's be the voice for the voiceless. Let's pray for God's healing to touch the hearts and minds of those we may not see, but know exist. We are not called to judge or retaliate, even when others are in the wrong, we are simply called to forgive, no matter how hard it may be. Now this doesn't mean you are to ignore or dismiss abuse or allow people to walk all over you or others, it means that hurt people will hurt people, just like we've discussed before, and there are deeper things going on. It means that forgiving them allows you freedom, because that burden of hate and revenge is not meant for your shoulders. My dad always found a reason to forgive.

Knowing how long my father was rejected, experiencing the injustice with my family, and seeing the constant mistreatment for as many years as I had, led to many internal struggles. It led to anxiety when returning to those settings, anxiety with leaving my father in places, and anxiety related to the pressure of feeling like I needed to be in my father's presence *all the time,* despite having a life of my own. But you see here friends, it's in those moments where we must rise above it all. Acknowledging your struggles, coping appropriately, and actively working on yourself is all part of the process. Being real allows you to heal. When I caught myself slipping down that dark tunnel of anxiety, I would meditate on this verse:

> *"Get rid of all bitterness, rage and anger, brawling and slander, along with every form of malice. Be kind and compassionate to one another, forgiving each other, just as in Christ God forgave you."*
>   (EPHESIANS 4:31-32 NIV)

It's easy, even tempting to think the worst, but kindly remind your heart and your head that hope and comfort in God is always available.

One of the hardest parts about being human is the idea of forgiveness. Forgiveness is just not human nature; it's God's nature. Psychologists generally define forgiveness as a deliberate, conscious decision to release vengeance or resentment toward a group or person who has harmed or hurt you, regardless of whether they deserve your forgiveness or not. There are no accidents or coincidences. God places specific people in your life for a reason and it's your duty to love them and forgive them. Your job isn't to change peoples' hearts or deliver justice; your job is to encourage those around you, it's God's job to do the rest.

If God had spoken to us about what was to come in our lives, I think we would've said, "um, no, we're good God, we definitely cannot handle all of that so can we just skip that part?" But God will never give us anything He doesn't think we are prepared to handle. I am so grateful that God has the wisdom and foresight to know when to give us what and guide us through, over, and around each obstacle. Though it may seem like these challenges are just being thrown at you left and right with a few unexpected curve balls, there is a game plan amidst the chaos. What we perceive as chaos, is simply God's plan with reason, we just might not see it yet. With all the pain and brokenness that our family endured, it would have been easy to think we were losing the game of life, but my friend, you really don't know how strong you can be until you have God's strength with you at bat. You can't lose with God. And when you have the strength to give your pain to God, no matter how big or small that hurt may be, you will restore your resilience. That is the beauty behind pain and forgiveness, it goes far beyond anything that can be measured because we are created in the image of God and He is infinite.

Call out for God's help and be real with God, He already knows everything you were, are, and have been. If you are mad, be mad. God wants to hear your soul when you pray. It's ok to be hurting, that's normal. All that hurt, setback, struggle, and injustice is what God wants to heal and restore. Invigorate your soul and allow Him to breathe life into your time here. Delight in His light, amplify the gratitude you have for Him and let it overflow into everything around you. Then watch your foundation become impenetrable as you withstand every battle the enemy intended for your destruction. There may be 10,000 reasons for you to give up, but there are just as many reasons for you to overcome. Trust me my friend, with every season there's a reason. SO BLESS THE LORD, AND WORSHIP HIS HOLY NAME.

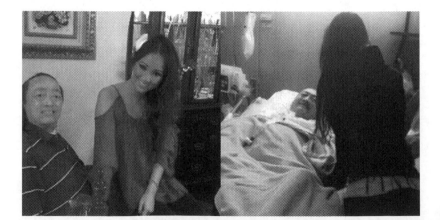

Chapter 17

Mark

Can you agree that God works in mysterious ways? We might not have all the reasons for why things happen, and we may never get the answers *we* want, but know that one day, when we are face-to-face with God, He will give us those answers. Living life depending on answers and demanding facts, defeats the whole purpose of God's intention for us. Faith is about believing the unseen, trusting in what God has provided us. We must trust that sometimes not knowing is what's best for us. We must walk by faith, not by sight. We must show our faith not by words, but by actions. Let faith be the reason you persevere, let faith be your reason to for hope, and let faith be your reason to find courage where it may not have been before.

It was possible for my dad; so, it IS possible for you, too.

My brother Mark and I are about a decade apart and before I was born, my brother had my dad all to himself. They did all the fun daddy-son activities you could imagine, from boy scouts and road trips to little adventures up to Mt. Laguna. That place was their favorite spot. The snow would delicately coat the mountain tops, carefully layering the world in white. That world, Mark's world with my dad, was so very different than mine. His world was filled with love from a physically healthy dad, but the grass is not always greener, the snow is not always whiter, and the world is not always brighter from a different side. He unfortunately also had to witness his strong father transition from being full of life to becoming depressed and sick. The type of pain him and I endured was night and day.

Mark was in high school when my dad's disease really began to take over. My dad, the doctor, became frustrated at his inability to "fix" the problem, despite his attempts to build up his immunity and be healthy again. One day at the mall, Mark was about fifteen years old and pushing my dad in his wheelchair when it became lodged in a crack, sending my dad tumbling forward onto the ground, in front of everyone. Mark dealt with all kinds of situations like this, he became my dad's caregiver when my mom had to work full time, he experienced adversity firsthand, and he somehow handled this all with grace. If roles were reversed, I honestly can't say whether or not I would have been able to manage that type of pain. God knows who needs what and when; only *he* knows.

Mark is generally shy and a man of few words; an introvert by nature. He was never really outwardly expressive when it came to emotions, that is, until my dad passed. During the last few days of my dad being on earth, while we were saying our goodbyes, Mark broke down. Really broke down. Through his tears he spilled his anger; his powerlessness at the outcome of our father's life, of our lives. In that moment, I saw his true vulnerability, I saw years of turmoil, I saw him as that little boy scout, innocent and excited for his next adventure with Dad. Only, this was not the adventure he had in mind. I could feel his frustration at the injustice of having a father who was paralyzed without a solution and then having that father taken from him. Why would God allow this to happen? Why could God heal others, but then not our Dad? He then apologized for not being there as much as he should've been. Hearing those words spoken, I had a vision. I imagined my dad's spirit standing next to my brother, hugging him and brushing away his tears. I imagined my dad right there, right there, in that moment, hovering over my brother, whispering to his younger boy scout self, "You were more than enough, my loving son." Mark, my one and only brother, gave an unforgettable speech at my dad's celebration of life, there wasn't a dry eye in the room. My brother, who never really said much, stood up in front of 500 people and opened up the wounds that accompanied years of loving my dad. Mark *loved* my dad and my dad undoubtedly loved Mark.

With grief it's interesting, there are moments that may not seem funny to someone on the outside, but when you're in it, all you can do is laugh. We had so many funny, family moments that could have been catastrophic but fortunately, became memorable laughs. There was this one time, before my dad had passed, where our family had the honor of speaking at a managerial conference in front of what we thought would be about twenty people, but what ended up being an audience of 600. I remember how nervous my dad was before speaking.

But it wasn't because of all the people or having to share his story, no, he was nervous about having enough oxygen in the tank to get through his speech. After my dad ended by saying, "YOU GUYS ARE THE BEST!" my sweet, loving mother and brother wheeled him off the stage. In their excitement, the wheelchair almost toppled off the ramp and would've taken all three with it. As if that wasn't enough excitement, after my brother gave his speech, every inch of his shy self-wanted to high tail it out of that room, unfortunately for him, his phone didn't accompany his haste. He begrudgingly had to turn his butt right back around, "sneak" back up to the front row and grab his phone in front of 600 unwavering eyes. We had a laugh about it later. Afterwards, between relief and happiness, there were some laughs about what could've happened. Thank God for those laughs, those are the moments that take us back to good times, those are our reasons.

Boys are so different than girls in soooooo many ways. Whenever I would visit my dad at the nursing home it was nonstop chatter about boys, the latest fashion, and whatever else was happening in life. He would always listen, eagerly awaiting my next question or story. But when Mark had his visits, they would both sit in silent contentment, enjoying the beautiful space between them. When they did talk, it would be about the newest version of electronics or sports, especially the Lakers; they shared the same obsession for the Los Angeles Lakers. They both had this resting "I'm good" face whenever they were together. Just as the bond between father and daughter is inseparable, so is the bond between father and son, it's just different. #DadSon.

My brother gave our dad three gifts. The first being the simple fact that Mark allowed him the ability to actually be a dad. He was the most amazing son a dad could ever ask for.

A son who was always there for his father, always present, and always faithful. Second, he gave the gift of grandfatherdom, or at least that's the word I invented to describe it. My father was granted the privilege of being a grandfather to his first, most precious grandson. He got to witness his son transition into fatherhood and become the best, most hardworking man for his three kids and wife. His last gift consisted of love. He was able to receive the most innocent love out there; the love of his three grandkids, Joshua, Addison, and Gabe. He was able to hear their tiny calls for grandpa, music to his ears.

As said before, God only gives us what we can handle, but let's be honest, there are moments in our lives that seem absolutely impossible to handle. God promises to get you through it and He got my brother through it. Today when I see my brother and his three kids, I'm reminded of all the love we shared with my dad.

There's a line from my brother's speech that has stuck with me over the years, "My dad knew my sister was ready, that he could leave this world. His job was done. I love you Dad. I can't wait to tell you all about how many championships the Lakers are going to win."

> *"And we know that God causes everything to work together for the good of those who love God and are called according to his purpose for them."*
> (ROMANS 8:28 NLT)

Trust God over your emotions. He knows what we can handle and what's best for us. Let us leave the world in confidence, knowing that God has our back. Knowing that we did our best to love, encourage, and inspire others as well as ourselves. Knowing that we were the person God had called us to be.

Less than one month after my dad's airway closed and he was intubated, then received a tracheostomy in 2012, Mark wrote a few words to share to his wife's blog. I decided to share it with you my friend, to give you a different perspective on the year that our lives shifted.

Thursday, December 6, 2012
There Were Better Days

It wasn't always this way...the fond memories of my dad growing up are those that I will cherish forever. I'm lucky to have been able to experience my dad spending time with me while he was still walking. He would take us to all these places. He drove us to Mt. Laguna to see snow and to San Francisco to see the Golden Gate Bridge. When I was younger, he would always take me to Boy Scouts and karate. I feel humbled to have been able to spend the time I had with my dad during his better years because when he got sick it started to get tough.

One summer, during the early stages of his illness, while my mom went to work, I stayed home just so I could keep my dad company during the day. They told me that if I stayed home all summer, they would buy me either a computer or a video game system. I chose a computer; I guess it was all worth it :). When I learned how to drive and my dad wanted to go to Fry's, Best Buy or UTC Mall, I would take him and that would always bring him joy. He loved going to the stores just to browse; most of the time we wouldn't buy anything. My dad just wanted to be out and about rather than being cooped up in the house all day and night. I never understood during my teenage years why this happened. I couldn't fathom the reality of his disease and why doctors couldn't find a cure. Perhaps I was too young to comprehend. Nonetheless, I wanted to blame someone or something but to no avail.

As the seconds turned to minutes and minutes turned to hours and hours turned to days and days turned to twenty-three years, I sit here today in my dad's hospital ICU room reminiscing about all the years that have passed. How did it come to this? Why did it come to this? Questions that may never be answered. Growing up was hard enough and seeing my dad suffer this way is even harder. My dad's will to live is something I admire. No matter how much he has endured all these years, even at the most trying time of his life, he is still fighting. Sitting here, I realize that the most important things in the world are the ones that are close at heart.

A professor of mine in college once shared a story about a jar filled with golf balls. He took an empty jar and filled it with several white golf balls and asked the class if it was full. Naturally everyone said yes. But my professor said no. He then filled it with small pebbles and asked again if it was full. We all said yes, but the answer was still no. He then filled it with sand and again asked if it was full. We all just stared in confusion. Some said yes and some said no. My professor said it was still not full. Lastly, he filled it with water and said now it is full. The story goes: the golf balls represent the main aspects of our lives, everything else that filled the jar is what fills our lives and makes it complete. He then asked the class, what do the golf balls mean to you? What about the rest of the components that made it full, what do those represent? The golf balls to me represent my family and children, everything else is my career, home, God etc.... but then thinking about it, are we really ever content with everything, are our lives ever complete? I guess not since it's an ever-changing world and every day something comes up. Something like what is happening now. All of a sudden, my jar feels somewhat empty.

Maybe I'll never understand what is going on and why this

ever happened. All I can do now is be positive and optimistic. For now, I will leave everything up to God. Dad I applaud you for your courage and valor. I'm here for you always. Thank you for everything!

Love, Mark - your son

Chapter 18

Walking Away

One of the toughest parts of that final day in my dad's hospital room, was leaving him lying there on the bed, lifeless. You are just expected to leave. As if it was nothing. Leave the father you loved behind. The man you called "dad" for twenty-seven years. Walking away when your mind is telling you to stay. When your heart is yelling at you to fight, to keep going. I don't remember that walk back to my car. I do remember trying to find my car, that took about an hour. I also remember almost driving back to the hospital that evening thinking he was still there. We as a family had to adapt to a "new" environment, a "new" way of thinking, a "new" normal.

I can't even count the times all of us drove to the nursing home, forgetting he was no longer there.

No more seeing my dad's name pop up on my phone. No more hospital chats or nursing home greetings. It all just abruptly stopped. It wasn't unexpected but at the same time it was, and I just couldn't wrap my brain around it. I remember driving back home after he passed and I had this surreal feeling, and truly believed, that my dad was in the car with me. I've never had to communicate with my dad through prayer because I had always texted him or called him. Now my only option was to listen and pray. And in the car, I *heard* him speak to me, "Hey, I'm here wherever you go now, just a prayer away, my sweet Hannah." At that moment I felt the gift unravel, the gift of my forever guardian angel. I love the saying that goes, "At first I was his angel, now he's mine." I actually have that as a keychain; a gift given to me on my dad's one-year death anniversary from my sweet and thoughtful cousin. As daughters, we are our dads' angels, despite being the little emotional creatures we can be, we are and will always be their precious angels. #GirlDad always HOORAY!

Since I had become so accustomed to visiting the hospital and nursing facilities, I didn't know how to fill that emptiness after my dad passed. During that transitional time, I heard of a girl who had the same disease that my dad had. She was in the early stages of GBS/CIDP and in a coma. Feeling desperate to hold onto some semblance of what my "normal" was before and sensing a need to continue visiting someone with the same illness, I had to see her. No idea who she was. Never met her. I just knew that I needed to visit her. I remember walking into the hospital and just sitting in her room, like a lost, empty soul. Why was I even here? What did I hope to get out of this? What could I say to her to help her? So many questions running through my mind. When she opened her eyes throughout the night, I would ask her if she needed anything, like I used to do for my dad. I had to rebuild my identity and who I was. I would often cry in her room; wishing it was still my dad lying there. I would close my eyes and hear the alarms, imagining it was my dad's monitor. I not only lost my dad —I lost myself.

I came to visit her consistently over the next few months. I never told her my story or that I was grieving my father who passed from the exact same heartbreaking disease she had. When she became somewhat alert, she asked, "Why have you been visiting me and who are you?" A very understandable question! I was asking myself the same thing. Who am I? Why am I here? I responded, "You know, to be honest, I'm not really sure. I just came for the chocolate pudding, I heard it was the best in town." She looked at me, and for the first time, laughed.

I continued to visit her and we talked about everything under the moon, especially our favorite topic, boys, ha. I got to visit her months later when she was recovering and had begun to walk again. I remember someone asking me if I was resentful that my dad never had that same opportunity. He was in that rare category of people affected by GBS/CIDP that were paralyzed for life. A majority of people with GBS/CIDP did indeed, walk again and recover from the disease. But not my dad. Was I resentful? Of course I was. I'm only human. I'm not a robot, I do have emotions. But that was a lesson that taught me to accept the situation and surrender to God. And I continued to battle through those tough emotions and insecurities with God by my side. You see friend, we don't live for answers, we live by faith. We must leave some answers in His hands. I learned how to empathize with those who were still suffering without allowing resentment to creep in.

I learned to rejoice with those who were recovering. If I had all my prayers answered, what faith would I need? I'd become arrogant and confident with an I-don't-need-you-God attitude.

What do you have to walk away from? What is hindering you from living your best life? Let others be your reason. Let *helping* others be your reason.

Walking away that afternoon, leaving my dad's room after he passed away, it felt like the end in so many ways. However, with God's grace, I am able to work on my healing and write about my experiences so that you may be encouraged during whatever season you're in. I had to choose whether to get better or be bitter; I chose better, I chose joy. I knew that the pain we went through over a twenty-seven-year period of time could not be wasted; it had to *mean* something. Just as I referenced earlier in the book, our biggest tests in life will become our testimonies. The whys and what-ifs may not be answered in the timely fashion we'd like, but have hope in knowing that God has a plan and that you are not alone. God sees. God hears. God loves. He doesn't promise that what we go through will be good, but He does promise that good will come from it. Pain, loss and grief will challenge your emotions; they will take you to the place of giving up. Don't give in to that feeling, the best is yet to come.

Transporting my dad's empty wheelchair felt like an out of body experience. I was in shock; I felt like I was just going through the motions. Every noise, every smell, every person reminded me of what I had just lost. Looking down at the wheelchair, seeing remnants of crumbs from my dad's meal only the day before, his blue tooth for his cell phone hanging off the side as if it was ready for him to take another call. The man who I adored, loved, looked up to, admired, laughed with, my best friend's chair, was now empty. I was in denial. Here is the truth my friend, God and my dad were there giving me the strength I needed to put one foot in front of the other that day. There's no other possible way I could have walked out of that facility on my strength alone.

"But he said to me, 'My grace is sufficient for you, for my power is made perfect in weakness.' Therefore, I will boast all the more gladly about my weaknesses, so that Christ's power may rest on me. That is why, for Christ's sake, I delight in weaknesses, in insults, in hardships, in persecutions, in difficulties. For when I am weak, then I am strong."

(2 CORINTHIANS 12:9-11 NIV)

Whatever unique challenges you are facing today, God uses change to change us. If everything around us stayed the same, how would we be able to grow? How would we be able to evolve into the person we are meant to be? Change allows us to enter into a new stretch of life and we can't do that if our life remains stagnant. Just like a heart rate monitor, if the line is straight, you're dead. But if it's moving up and down, you're alive, you're amongst the living. Walking through those feelings of hopelessness and walking away from seasons of your life that need to end, is what gives you the power to start a new beginning. Pray that God allows you the strength to renew, to transform, to walk into an entirely different mindset. Pray that He breathes life into your new passions, your new strategies for coping, your new discomfort so that it may transform into comfort; pray that He will help you to look forward. Looking back will only give you a sore neck. Walk with God. Walk the runway of life like you own it; purposefully and meaningfully.

#GirlDad

Principle Seven

REMEMBERING HIS LOVE FOR YOU

Chapter 19

TBT-Let's Throw it Back

For anyone unfamiliar with the phrase "TBT" it means: Throw Back Thursday. I'm a millennial so acronyms are just another day in the life for me. I felt it was only appropriate for you to not just see *my* reasons for life, my raw emotions, and my walk with God on this journey, but also the perspectives from those that I love. So as promised, I've included journal entries from family members that divulge the difficulties and joys of our time together with my dad. As a family, we were so emotionally drained from everything that updating everyone on my dad's health became another hurdle. Fortunately, my sister in law, Grace, started a blog to document our struggles. Interesting fact, my brother and Grace have been together since 8th grade and they are now forty-one years old. Yup, they are that rare couple that succeeded as little kid sweethearts. Grace relates to our loss because she too experienced losing her father. We are so grateful that she had the know-with-all to write everything down so we could look at it later and now, share it with you.

I know how important it is to stay present, but sometimes I feel it's just as important to reflect on the past. As I read back on these entries, it has not only brought me encouragement, but also revealed how much we've overcome. Those times we thought life wouldn't get better; that it was the end, turned out to be one of many new beginnings.

Our 2012 family Thanksgiving is a perfect example of that. It was the day my dad's airway closed, forcing him to be placed on a tracheostomy and in turn, transferred from the comforts of his own home to a nursing facility. It was necessary in order for my dad to continue to live. That marked tragedy forever changed our family, but it was also a reminder of God's promise to never leave us or forsake us. Who knew my dad would never be able to come live back at home? His new home would be nursing facilities and hospitals. The physician had informed us that if we decided to trach him, his quality of life would be poor, that it would be a life not worth living. As a family, these difficult decisions took a lot of courage and even more faith in God. I already knew everything that would come with trach care because a few months prior to this incident, I was still in school for respiratory therapy. I was quite aware of the hardships we were about to endure. But my dad went on to live six, solid years. Six more beautiful years of love. Six more years of him hearing me say "Dad" and me getting to say it. Six more years of being a husband. Six more years of embracing his grandchildren. Six more years of miracles. Six more years of laughter.

When all the odds are against you and the risks are high, take that chance without hesitation. Live for your family. Love for your family. Fight for your family. Even now, as I reflect on my dad's passing almost two years ago, I thought that was the end for me as well, but it was just the start of a new normal. It was the start of my fight to find myself. It was our fight, as a family, to heal. As you read along, just know with confidence that what might seem like the end is just the beginning. Stand strong, be courageous, and don't lose sight of your reasons to keep going. Truly, the best is yet to come.

The blog you're about to read is from when I was twenty-two, forgive the grammar mistakes, but I wanted to keep it as authentic as possible.

Monday, December 3, 2012
The Man Who Never Stops Fighting

"You never know what you got until its gone", is a saying that I've always heard but never really understood until now. My Dad has been a big part of my life since I was born, I might've not truly been able to see that than I can see that now. He has been paralyzed for 23 years and I am currently 22. These past 2 weeks from the morning of Thanksgiving 2012 until today December 3, 2012, the one thing that seems to be a big heartache is not having my Dads presence at home. Every day the first person I would see would be my Dad. My Dad was always present at the house, his joy was to get some fresh air while listening to Gods word. When you see your loved one sick you want nothing more than to help them and be there for them and really think back on the times you spent with him and how you should've been there more often for him. What I didn't realize was that the one person who truly cared and wanted nothing but the best, was by my side the whole time.

My Dad has been nothing but fighting for his life to live every day to see the one he loves grow and be a family. My Dad wants to live, no medication no disease no illness no ONE can stop by dads growing desire to live. I remember the one thing my dad would ALWAYS say to me on a daily basis besides "I love you forever and ever", he would always tell me " Hannah, God is good" with a very weird smile he always put on haha. To be someone who has been sick and had the whole world ahead of him and for it all to be taken away in a blink of an eye, that person is sitting her telling me that "God is good", has taught me more than any devotional book has ever taught me; God will provide peace to those who seek. He has been breathing through a TRACH located in his throat which provides his breathing for him through a Mech Vent (life support). All Vitals have been pretty stable in the normal range, he has been receiving Trach Care, Breathing Treatments, In-line feeding and endless love from his family. The one thing the Doctors and nurses have been saying since the day he was admitted is that, "Doctors are the worst patient", haha. Love you forever and ever Dad :]

-Your spoiled Princess, HANNAH

Thursday, November 2012
Mary Did you know?

The holidays were fast approaching during the warm Fall season. Thanksgiving was around the corner. People were beginning to plan out their menus and decorations were blanketing the stores everywhere. I placed an olive colored tablecloth on our dining table. In the center I placed three maple shaped place mats that is reminiscent of the colors you would see during the Fall season on trees in the east coast. The burnt orange, dark green and deep red color reminded me of how much this time of the year brings so much love and joy in everyone.

I love the smell of Thanksgiving. The different herbs infused in the different dishes that are being cooked up on the stove and baked in the oven fills the house. I usually start cooking early in the morning and have Thanksgiving lunch at our house. We then spend the rest of this day at the Martin's house. Although, this last year was a bit different.

The night before, Mark and I went to the store to gather up all the ingredients that I was going to need. The big question was whether to get roast beef or ham. The winner was roast beef, I was glad because I love meat. Before heading home, we stopped by Mom & Dad's house. When we opened the door, we were immediately greeted by all of Mom's dogs. They were her little darlings; like her little children. Dad looked lethargic, his eyes a bit swollen. You could see weakness in his face. Dad had taken prescribed medicine that was causing him to become limp. We told Dad he should get some rest and drink lots of water that night. Before we left for home, we discussed our plans for Thanksgiving. This year we would do lunch at the Martin's. Mom said she would just bring bibingka that she would buy from a local store. Bibingkas are a rice cake made with coconut milk wrapped in a banana leaf and cooked over heated coal. It's like a Filipino version of the bread pudding but better in my opinion.

I was excited not to have to wake up so early on Thanksgiving Day. We headed over to the Martin's around noon just before the football game was to start. When we pulled up to the driveway, we noticed that Mom and Dad's van was not there. Unbeknownst to us, we walked right in and were greeted by everyone already sitting around the living room watching the game. I scanned the room but did not see Mom and Dad. While getting food, we were told that Dad went to the emergency. Suddenly the festive day turned into a somber celebration. This was the first year that we didn't spend this holiday with Mom and Dad. Mark left early to go to the hospital. I left to go home shortly after.

While at the hospital Mark updated me on Dad's condition. This time it wasn't looking good. Dad's CO2 level was high, and he was going to need to be admitted. This marked the day of the rest of our lives and how life was going to be for now on. In just a blink of an eye our life turned upside down and a whirlwind of unknowns was in our future.

If the only thing you needed to worry about was choosing between ham or roast beef then I would take that over what we have now. Oh, Mary did you know that one day it would be like this? When life hands you lemons then you make lemonade. It's been 23 years, do we stop here and give up or do we take what we have and make the best out of it? Mom, took those lemons and made 23 years' worth of lemonades. Though some of it were bittersweet and some were the best times, nonetheless we can't look back or turn back time. What we have today is God's plan for our lives. Whether it's good or bad, there are always reasons to why we are in the situations were are in. It makes us stronger and wiser.

-Grace Joya

Saturday, December 1, 2012
God is Good

> *"The Lord is good; His mercy is everlasting, And His*
> *truth endures to all generations."*
>
> (PSALMS 100:5 NKJV)

Last couple of days have been a blur for both Dad and the family. Dad is finally off sedation and can now process everything that has happened.

(Flashback) On November 22, 2012, Thanksgiving Day just before heading out to spend this day with family, Dad fainted. On Sunday late night early Monday November 26 at about 3:45am he coded blue and was intubated. We thank God for another day. On Tuesday November 27 Dad had a Tracheostomy. The procedure went well.

Today is December 1, 2012, 25 days 'til Christmas. We are all here to support Dad and help with the trials and tribulations. With the tracheostomy we now have a new battle to face. Learning to read lips.

Just now the Respiratory Therapists examined Dad and tried to have him breathe without the help of the ventilator. We tried for about 15 minutes but had to go back to the machine. Tomorrow they will try again. After the trial Dad was telling us something but we had a hard time understanding. I wanted to cry but knew I had to be strong for him. It felt like an eternity to finally figure out what he was trying to say. We put a straw in his mouth while he pointed to the letters and after some struggle, we figured it out. He wanted to know if the nurse knew how to do something. It was both a relief and an exciting feeling and somewhat confusing. I didn't know how I should have felt. At times I wanted to speak for him because I saw the tears trickling down his face. All I could think of during the moments he was trying to communicate with us was, we are going to get thru this.... We are going to make it... This is just a road bump... Another crazy atomic bomb that was dropped in the Joya household.

Sometimes we take things for granted and I realized today that I have so much to be thankful for. So much to be grateful for.... Sometimes we don't know how lucky we JUST are...

-Grace Joya

Sunday, December 2, 2012
Before today...

Dad had many hopes and dreams when he finished medical school in the Philippines. After practicing medicine for several years, he migrated his family to America in the early 1980's where he would continue with his profession of being a medical doctor. Coming to the U.S. was supposed to be a fulfilling adventure of prosperity and to live the American Dream. However, that dream was shattered 23 years ago when Dad came down with the common flu.

A couple days went by and he got somewhat better but was still sick. Sadly, he never got better from what we believed was caused by the flu. An illness that millions of people across the United States come in contact with every year. Throughout the years doctors tested and treated him for what they believe is a rare disease called Chronic Inflammatory Demyelinating Polyneuropathy (CIDP).

According to the New England Journal of Medicine, CIDP is an under diagnosed disease that is potentially treatable affecting 1 to 100,000 adults.

A little math break if you will:

There are 6,973,738,433 people in the world (Google.com)

That means there are approximately 69,737 people in world who have this disease.

And if there are 196 countries in the world then there are about 355 people per country who have this disease.

If you break it down even further only 7 people per (U.S.) state are suffering from this disease.

CIDP is often compared to another form of disease called Guillen-Barre Syndrome. CIDP is a neurological disorder that leads to progressive weakness that disables sensory functions in the legs and arms. The body's immune system attacks its own nerves and gradually destroys it and eventually the ability for the nerves to perform worsens. There are several treatments that can help lessen the burden of CIDP but there is unfortunately no cure.

Present day...

For the last 23 years Mom has been taking care of him. His illness progressed quickly, and he lost the ability to walk, stand and do everyday chores. I lived with them for 4 years and witnessed first -hand the hardship. Mom would wake up very early in the morning before going to work to prepare food and bathe Dad. I watched how she would transfer Dad from the bed to the wheelchair and from the wheelchair to the shower chair and back to the wheelchair. Before they got the accessible van, she would even lift him up and transfer him inside the car. Without any hoist or help from a lift machine, Mom did all this for the last 23 years. If that wasn't enough work, she also had a full-time job and was a full-time mom to a son and daughter. She's one amazing and strong woman.

For the last year, Dad's condition had worsened. His breathing deteriorated and he required a BiPAP machine, which is a breathing apparatus to help get more air in and out of his lungs. In the last year he has been confined to his electric wheelchair where he sleeps and stays 24/7 because he has deteriorated so much.

This is how we got to where we are today... And yet there are still more struggles, more trials and more to come. The unknown is inevitable.

–Grace Joya

Monday, December 3, 2012
Straw

"Have you ever wondered what it felt like to be paralyzed from the neck down? Now imagine being paralyzed neck down, not being able to talk, eat or drink.

Let's play a little game...Try this in front of someone if you are able to. Ok...think for a moment that both of your hands are tied together, sit in your chair and stay still. Now, while staying still pretend like you can't speak, sort of like you have a bad case of laryngitis. Move your mouth without making any sounds and tell the other person that you want a drink. Say this phrase like how you would normally talk, "Can you get me water please?" Let's take it a little further this time. Now put a straw or pencil in your mouth. Take a piece of paper and write the alphabet on it. Now using your pencil or straw in your mouth point to the letters one by one while the other person holds up the paper for you. REMEMBER, you are paralyzed from the neck down and can only move your head. Spell out what you wanted to say. Now imagine you're the other person at the other end trying to figure out what you are trying to say. Imagine doing this all night and day for 2 days straight with no sleep or rest. How's that for a visual, huh?

On Sunday December 2, Mark (Dad's son & my husband) called me at around 4 pm. He was at the hospital and asked me to go to there because Dad was trying to say something and Mom, Hannah (Dad's daughter) and he could not figure it out. The night before Mark and I figured out how to somewhat communicate with Dad. We put a straw in his mouth and had him point to each letter on a paper that I had made for him. The paper had all 26 letters of the alphabet on it. Dad seemed ecstatic because now he could say the things, he wanted to tell us instead of us trying to read his lips, which at times was easy and other times extremely difficult. It took nearly half an hour to figure out one sentence that only had I think 5 words. In my head I was thinking, God please just create a miracle and give him his voice back already, I don't know how long more I can do this for. We did this for almost 4 hours, communicating this way. I stood there while he pointed to the letters and Mark wrote them down on another piece of paper so we could keep track. Mark and I took turns for 4 hours doing this. When Mom came back to the hospital after going home to freshen up, we told her what we discovered. She was happy when we showed it to her but didn't realize what was to come of that night. We left the hospital at about 10 pm so Mom and Dad could rest. That's what we thought happened.

Sunday, Dec 2 was the day we all broke down. Mom hadn't slept now for 9 days since Dad went into the hospital. Her eyes are so swollen I can't even see her pupils anymore. Last night when she thought she was going sleep she didn't. She stayed up all night while Dad talked to her pointing to each letter on the paper and with the straw in his mouth.

It is now Sunday night; Dad again was trying to tell us something, but we could not make it out. We all got agitated and inpatient with him. We wrote down each letter one by one but still could not figure it out. Finally, after several attempts and 3 hours later we got some words. About 10 or so words. Just words though because we couldn't put it together to make a sentence. It is like a huge jigsaw puzzle; you just want to finish it but there are a gazillion pieces. All the while doctors, nurses and the respiratory therapists were all coming by to check on him because his heart rate went up to 130+, his saturation was low and on top of it all he had a high fever and an infection. At times he would ignore the medical staff so he can point to the letters. I stood there while the nurse worked around me to drain his IV and do a physical exam. The respiratory therapist came by and did what he had to do but Dad was still at it, the doctors also came by and still Dad was at it. Anytime the medical staff would try and take out the straw from his mouth he would move his head back and forth and away from them. At this point Mom, Mark, Hannah and I were at our wits end. We didn't know what to do anymore and made a decision to grab all of our stuff and go into the waiting room so the nurses could take care of Dad and do what they had to do.

In the waiting room...all four of us sat there voicing our concerns and frustrations. None of was probably at the right state of mind at the moment. At least for me, no matter how calm I was, inside I wanted to blow up and scream. I can't even imagine how Mom was feeling or thinking. Mark on the other hand seemed drained and exhausted as well. Hannah was the same way. We all asked each other if doing the Tracheostomy was the right decision. We all questioned Dad's medical state of condition. How long are we each going to be able to handle this? Are we going to make it through this? Mom cried, screamed and sighed. I didn't know how to comfort her or what to say to her. I know she is extremely stressed and tired. We all sat in the waiting for about 30 minutes before heading home. We didn't go back into the room anymore because we wanted Dad to rest. He seemed to calm down, so we all headed home hoping for a good night rest 'til the next day."

-Grace Joya

Tuesday, December 11, 2012
Today...our first Christmas as a family in the hospital

> *"For God so loved the world that he gave his one and only Son, that whoever believes in him shall not perish but have eternal life".*
>
> JOHN 3:16 (NIV)

It's been a few days since I last saw my Father in Law, Dad, and wrote about his status. The last couple days has given us hope that everything will be better. Dad has shown some progress. He is still in ICU and is still fighting.

During the last few days he has been battling pneumonia that he just can't shake off. The doctors have been treating him with a strong antibiotic and even sedated him at one point in order to clear his lungs. He's had a low-grade fever as well as high grade fevers. His blood pressure has also fluctuated, and his CO_2 was also of concerned. Nevertheless, every time Mark came home, he would to tell me how Dad was doing; he is doing just fine, no changes – he would tell me. Until of course today...

When Mark and I stepped into his hospital room, we were welcomed with an overwhelming feeling that is hard to explain. One RT was pumping a bag that was attached to his trach. The bag was oxygen so he can breathe while the other RT did what she needed to do in order to stabilize his oxygen levels. Dad's CO_2 levels were in a dangerous state, triple the normal amount anyone should have. The other nurse was working on all his IV lines and the doctor just supervising at the moment making sure everything was going fine. I could see Dad's head shaking, his eyes staring into the wall. You know there was something wrong. The doctor then performed a procedure called bronchoscopy to examine his lungs. The doctor took a sample that he will send to the lab for tests. After the procedure, the doctor informed us that Dad's lungs were like hard sponge like material. They were no longer pumping the way it should be. His diaphragm was also paralyzed now and that was causing his CO_2 level to increase to dangerous levels. Even though the tracheostomy was supposed to help with his breathing, it doesn't look like at this point that is case. The doctor has given him steroids for his lungs and another medicine to treat his pneumonia. The doctor seemed optimistic and said he will do everything he can for Dad until we go to the next step.

We entered the room again after the procedure. Dad looks scared, tired, in pain and his head shaking. He feels hot but his body feels cold to the touch. His CO_2 still high but at least he's stabilized for now.

At times you wonder how long more he will have to suffer. He can't breathe on his own and needs the ventilator, he can't eat and requires a feeding tube, he can't speak because of the trach and he can't move because of his disease. As I leave the hospital today I says goodbye to Dad until the next time we seem again...

For now, here are some pictures of his hospital room. We made it look like Christmas. Until then...

Still in ICU.

-Grace Joya

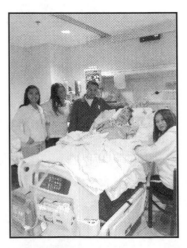 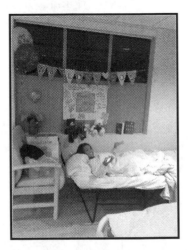

Merry Christmas

I am honestly so thankful that Grace was able to be proactive during a time when our family could not think further than the moment. When I read the blog, for a split second I can't imagine someone having to go through all of that and then I snap back to reality, realizing that "someone" was my dad. I remember thinking that would be the last night I would see my dad. But God was not finished with him yet.

Friends, you don't need a big 'ol mansion with snowflakes falling, lights glistening and presents everywhere to experience the true joy of Christmas. For us, Christmas was simply spending time together, wherever that may be. We didn't have Christmas carolers or holiday tunes or lavish decorations, (unless you count the hospital alarms and heart rate monitors incessantly ringing and blinking) nor did we have stacks of gifts, but we did have each other, and that was most important gift of all. Being present was our present because life is a gift; the ultimate gift.

My prayer for you, as you finished those last few entries and experienced the turmoil with our family, is that you feel inspired. I know that sounds crazy, like the exact opposite of what you should be feeling, but I truly want you to feel encouraged in knowing that whatever rocky, rock bottom you may be at, you can, and *you will* overcome that obstacle. God's love and strength always guided us through the rough terrain. He guided us along a path of healing that *you will* discover in time. This next post is from 2013 and my whole family contributed. It was a time when everything was new to us. We were adjusting to a new normal, a new reality, a new life. Everything seemed impossible at that time. But God will not just get you over it, He will get you *through* it. Whatever season you are in today, allow yourself to feel the emotions through the motions; allow God's healing hands to take hold and guide you, helping you find the purpose through the pain. Now back to the blasts from the past, my friend. But before you continue on, go outside for a few minutes, breath some fresh air, say five things you're thankful for and we shall talk again soon. Peace out brussels sprout!

Monday, January 7, 2013
All Things Become New

They say pain is only temporary. That's what they say but is it really temporary? When you get a cut, it heals. When you break your bone, the doctors put a cast and it heals. When you get a cold, you take medicine and you heal. How about when you lose your vocal cords and your ability to eat, can you heal from that?

The last time I wrote Dad was still in ICU recovering from the tracheostomy procedure. He was also fighting infectious life-threatening illnesses. Christmas and New Years have come and gone. And today is now 2013.

So far God has blessed our family with another year to be able to spend with Dad. December was quite a hectic month and I couldn't find the time to write. Mom and Mark finally went back to work about 2 weeks after Dad was admitted to the hospital. Getting some normalcy back into our lives was good for the soul. Then about 2-3 weeks after being transferred to another Hospital, Dad was moved out of ICU and into a private room. This was a good sign. This meant that Dad's pneumonia was gone and no longer a threat to his health. It also meant that he was out of the danger zone and moving towards recovery. The doctors also began testing Dad's ability to swallow and by Christmas he was able to start eating small ice chips. Things were moving along, and we were slowly beginning to see him live again.

The past few Christmas we usually spend it at the Martin's (Auntie Maggie & Uncle Ray) house but this time was a bit different. This year Hannah and Mom spent it at what we call our "second house", the hospital. Mark, myself and the kids went to church Christmas Eve then went to the Martin's to celebrate. When we were opening up presents and doing our white elephant, we FaceTime'd Dad at the hospital. It was as if they were all there with us. Technology is definitely a work of wonder. On Christmas Day Mark went to the hospital and spent nearly the whole day with Dad, Mom and Hannah. If that wasn't enough of a Christmas surprise even Uncle Ray, Auntie Maggie, Jonathan and Elizabeth came by before going to watch a movie. Even Uncle Rick and Auntie Marcela came by as well. This was undeniably a Christmas we'll never forget. God gave us the best gift we could ask for and that was to spend it with Dad.

A few days past and New Year's Eve came. We all decided to spend this day with Dad at the hospital. Mark and I went to Party City and got some goodies and before going to the hospital we got Chinese food at this local restaurant called Hong Kong. We took it up to his room where Mom, Hannah, Mark, myself and the kids ate just before ringing in 2013. Our celebration even included a toast of Martinelli's apple cider and horns. Good thing we were at the end of the hall because we were so loud, but hey it's New Year's, right? Why not?

After the new year, Dad began drinking thickened liquids and eventually ground up foods. He also was able to get out of bed with the help of a hoist and onto a manual wheelchair. On January 3 he was able to drink soda, a beverage he prefers most. Then on January 5, we met with a representative from a company that specializes in speech for people with little or no mobility and those without a voice box due to a trach. The representative showed us how Dad would be able to communicate with a laptop computer and a mouse hooked up to his wheelchair. Since Dad is not able to move from his neck down, he would use his head to move the mouse around. The device is called EZ Keys, by using this program he is able to fully express himself and navigate the computer and Internet.

Although a lot of good things have come our way since this ordeal, Dad still is not able to go home and may never be able to. But who said we can't have two homes right? A home doesn't need to have 4 bedrooms a kitchen and a living room. A home just needs to be filled with the people you love. So, here's to 2013 and A happy new year!

-Grace Joya

Tuesday, February 5, 2013
Through the Looking Glass

When I marvel about all the blessings God has given me, I smile. Today I can sit here in front of my computer and enlighten you. Though I'm not complaining I must confess that until last month I never knew how privileged I really am. How privileged each of us are.

Dad was recently transferred down to a sub-acute rehabilitation hospital. There he would stay long term and be in the care of nurses who have been caregivers to patients that are bed ridden for years. Some even ten years or more. The move gave us an abundance of anxiety. Where was this new place Dad was being moved to? Is it safe there? Are the nurses as articulate and proficient? How is this change going to affect our lives? We had a lot of unanswered questions and were overpowered with emotions. Everything happened as if lightening had struck not once but twice. Not because we were stricken with good fortune but rather misfortune. A metaphor if you will.

When I saw Dad at this new place I was flabbergasted. I felt like I was knocked down by a crushing uppercut in the first round. I wouldn't even dare to call this place our "second home". I was blown away for sure. I tried to imagine the good things in life while I was there, but it was extremely difficult. I was overwhelmed, I wanted to cry, get mad, scream and do something right then and there. We were moving forward just a few days ago. Dad was getting better. He started eating, sitting and he was going to be able to talk using a machine. Instead, everything seemed to be moving backwards, as if we've time-warped back to the day he went into the ER. It was Thanksgiving all over again.

Dad's eyes were distended, his face frail. He looked like a wilted flower that was never given water, shriveled and hobbled over. His trach tube was being kept up by a clear plastic garbage bag that was tied to a wire rack on the wall. The machine they used looked like something from the 1950's. It even sounds like a lawn mower when the RT turned it on. To top it all off, the entire facility didn't have a single computer or internet connection. I was surprised they had cable. Is this the Twilight Zone? If it is, someone pinch me so I can wake up from this nightmare.

You ask why and so do we. I asked myself how I could ever come back to this repulsive place. After about half an hour I stepped out of his room and walked the hallways to the living area slash physical therapy room. I gasped with disbelief that this area looked a lot better than the patient rooms. After a few minutes there I needed fresh air so I went into the courtyard or should I say prison yard. If you've ever been to Alcatraz Island this place looks exactly like the courtyard where the prison mates would gather around to congregate and mingle. It was located in the middle of the entire facility. Imagine a big box with an open space in the middle and bright spotlights around the perimeter echoing imaginary guards hovering over.

Walking back to Dad's room I was able to catch a glimpse of some of the patients. They all seemed like unforgotten lifeless souls. Two doors down was a lady that had a stroke, across were two young boys and a few more doors down was a little old delicate lady just sitting in her chair. Dad's roommate was an old man who was also bed ridden. He too has a trach like Dad and had little mobility. Mom befriended this old man next to Dad. I think he was very happy that we were there because he doesn't have family in the U.S. His wife, passing a year before in the same facility was his closest kin. His children are in another country and the last time a family member had visited him was at least a few years ago. It is mindboggling how and why all this can happen to anyone.

I couldn't bear to stay in Dad's room not because I was sensitive to the hideous smell of human matter or felt claustrophobic in his prison-like cell they call a room but because I was uneasy. Hospital rooms have become second nature to me since Dad was admitted but this time was different. There was no room to breathe, the room was stuffy and there was a pungent odor that lingered. There wasn't a suitable explanation for my behavior. I just couldn't and didn't want to see Dad in his current state because it was too painful to witness.

As hypocritical as I want to be at this moment, I know that God has a plan for each of us. He teaches us not to worry because he has everything under control. When we can no longer cope, we should trust in Him.

—With every hope there is a future, live in the moment and take a mental picture because tomorrow is another day...

-Grace Joya

That was the last post written by Grace in 2013. After this post, our family really didn't have time to write about our experiences, we were just living them. For the next six years, we were on the craziest ride of our lives, no manual, no instructions, just a buckle in case we crashed. We learned to continue to trust God on our journey; allowing His loving hands to heal us and His light to guide us through what we would soon find out to be, our darkest days.

> *"Even though I walk through the darkest valley, I will fear no evil, for you are with me; your rod and your staff, they comfort me."*
>
> (PSALMS 23:4 NIV)

November 16, 1998 I was only 8 years old when I started writing about my Dad. The two images at the top are just a few journal entries I saved.

True love never dies

The 2 beautiful images on the top are hand drawn
designs by Max himself. My dads' best friend.

Chapter 20

Mahalo

The last vacation with my dad was in 2010 when we went to Hawaii. A few years back he texted me, saying that we would return to Hawaii when he got better. What we didn't know then, was that he would not be returning to that little slice of paradise on earth but instead, he'd be going to the ultimate paradise in Heaven.

Because of my dad's illness, he was often times looked at as less than a person. People would stare at him and treat him as his body looked, a sick, paralyzed, disabled man. Just a nobody to the world. But in God's eyes, he was a somebody. God was a carpenter by trade, He naturally fixes things that are broken. He has the ability to take what the world may see as crippled and transform it into a beautiful masterpiece. Let Him work His love on you.

I love what Pastor Rick Warren wrote in his book *The Purpose Driven Life*, "Your weaknesses are not an accident. God deliberately allows them in your life for the purpose of demonstrating His power through you. He is drawn to people who are weak." When we are weak, God is strong.

Even though we weren't able to travel any more with my dad, God had His very own idea of how to bring travel to us. While my dad was living in a nursing home, my mom had an extra room at the house, so she started hosting exchange students from all over the world. We had people from Germany,

Switzerland, Japan, and China staying with us. They became family. They would bring different types of gifts from their countries to give to my dad. He got a "taste of the world" even when he hadn't expected it. You see, God has our back. My dad got to experience different languages, cultures, and foods without leaving his room! He would get so excited to learn from what these students had to offer. Everyone is placed in our life to teach us something.

One day I will get to enjoy the paradise of Heaven with my father, eating fresh coconuts, devouring some bbq chicken... what?! I'm hungry! But in all seriousness, there is so much to be thankful for and God has provided time and time again, even when it was something we had no idea we needed. We needed to travel, even if it was only in our imagination through someone else's lens. As a family, vacations were more than just going somewhere, they were an opportunity for us to experience the world together. We may not have gotten to travel to Hawaii with my dad again, but we gained so much by listening to others and listening to God. Our world looked a little different sometimes, but I'm no less grateful for all the sweet experiences.

Mahalo #Ohana.

Chapter 21

Furry Friends

They always say a dog is a man's best friend…well we had lots of friends then. Some people would call our house a "farm" because we had a total of five dogs, six cats, four birds, and a lizard. My mom was feeding and caring for them all, as well as the birds outside…oh and did I mention the mice in the garage? Allow me to introduce our little furry familia starting with our youngest pup Chase, also known as a mini-samoan saint bernard. Next is Chanel who's known as the rockstar-hulk-mini-wild-bull. Then we've got Chance, our Chewbacca child straight from Star Wars. There's Coco, the three-pound tap dancer, ready to be on *Dancing With the Stars* and Mocha who's a class-act chihuahua graduate from Stanford

Law School. And finally, the kitty-cats: Nemo, Simba, Carmel, Raider, and Leilani. Welcome to the Joya farm.

When we would bring any of the lil' munchkins to the nursing home, it brought a little bit of home to my dad and joy to the other residents. One of our dogs, Coco, was my dad's dog. Coco would follow him all the time and always wanted to sit in his lap. When my dad would come home for a few hours, Coco was the most excited of all the furry friends, so much so, that his excitement would inevitably lead to a fit of sneezes. We all had our favorites. Mine was Mocha, who is still alive today, at twenty years old. Yup, *twenty* years old. The two other mini saint Bernard look a like's are both Mocha and Chances little fur babies. My mom's favorite was Chewbacca Chance, our fuzz ball.

One late evening when my dad came home for three hours, he went outside with Coco. When he came back inside, Coco hadn't followed. All of a sudden, we heard a blood curdling scream that probably woke up the whole neighborhood…a coyote had come up and snatched Coco in a split second. We were all devastated but my parents were inconsolable. RIP Coco. Fast forward six years and guess what? Another coyote attack. Our sweet Chance is at the vet, post-surgery after a brutal attack. Yesterday morning around 7 a.m., I was awakened by a dreadfully, loud scream. I knew that scream, I had heard it before when our 'lil Coco was attacked and taken away by a pack of coyotes in a matter of seconds. I ran to the kitchen to see my mom screaming and banging on the windows as a pack of coyotes approached three of our munchkins in the backyard. Chase and Chanel were frantically barking as Chance lay on the ground, lifeless. They were outside for less than 5min. My mom yelled, "CHANCE!!" and he popped up, giving the rest of us a near heart attack from his resurrection, and sprinted inside. He ran right into his bed and was acting a little dazed, we thought maybe it was from the shock of his ordeal. But then Chase began to lick his neck and Chance coughed up some blood. He sacrificed his own life to protect his kiddos from the coyotes.

There's never a dull moment on the farm…Chanel, our fighting girl, didn't want to be left out of any drama. About a few months back, she lost all nerve function in her back legs. My mom and I were devastated. The vet told us she would never be able to walk again. Once again, we as a family never gave up. We were determined to defeat the odds, just like we did with my dad. Every morning and night my mom would use a scarf as a harness and help Chanel elevate her back legs so she could walk with her front ones. My mom gave her nightly massages and I would give her words of affirmation. It wasn't even four months and our Chanel got up on her own and started walking. Resilience is contagious, even with our fur family.

My mom, also known as the "animal whisperer" always kept all the animals healthy and gave them lots of TLC (tender, love and care).

They say Heaven is a place of laughter. Dogs bring so much laughter and joy and if all dogs went to Heaven, my dad's lil Coco and him would have had the sweetest reunion.

When my dad was still living at home and Mocha was only two years old, she got stung by a bee. She fell on the floor, blocking my dad's pathway for his wheelchair. When he noticed that she looked somewhat swollen, he was unable to leave his room for a whole day to grab his phone. Thankfully, Mocha's bee sting was minor and she woke up like nothing happened. She went to many soccer games with my dad and was always riding first class in Dad's lap. Mocha is my dog; she doesn't take her eyes off me and follows me everywhere I go #clingy.

We were never really "cat people" but after we got the first kitten, there was no stopping us #crazycatwoman. Our sweet Carmel, who my mom called "the follower" but I deemed as "the stalker" just couldn't let the dogs have all the fun so get ready for a crazy cat story that still blows our minds to this day.

Whenever we visited my dad at the Carmel Mountain nursing home, my mom always spotted this baby, black kitten. My mom has a big heart for people, but an even bigger heart for animals. If she could have her own farm in Texas, she would've in a heartbeat. As days passed, my mom gave the black kitten the name Carmel. Whenever my mom and dad would have a date night outside the front porch at the nursing facility, Carmel would third wheel it. Our house was about ten minutes away, and one day Carmel decided to follow us home. Like, I'm not kidding, this little cat literally trotted from the nursing home to our house. We aren't really sure how she did it, but she did. In the months it took her to find our place, Carmel had a little date of her own, unbeknownst to us. When she arrived at our house, she gave birth to a litter of kittens. We decided to keep Carmel and one of the kittens, who we named Simba.

No one really knows what Heaven is like, we can only speculate. I believe we will see animals in Heaven. God so loved the world that He gave us furry friends. Have you ever really looked, I mean really, really looked at your pet? Notice all the minute details, the intricate fur designs, the way they move, God created that! Talk about a fun job! I believe whole-heartedly that the love you share with your furry friends continues on in Heaven. God wants us to enjoy this life and animals are a part of that happiness.

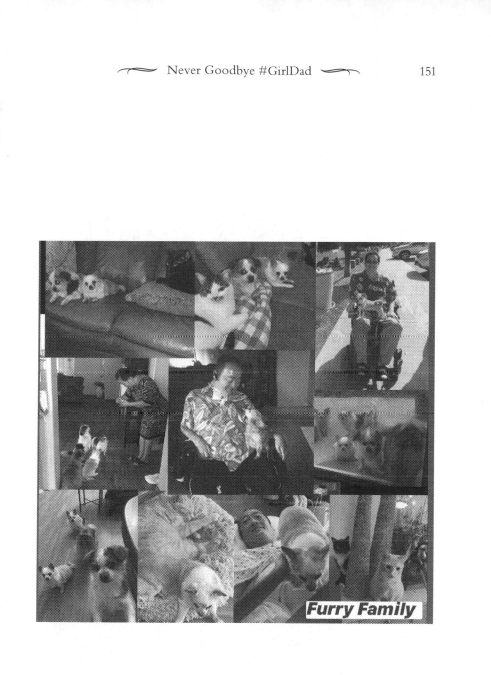

Furry Family

#GirlDad

Principle Eight

SETBACKS BECOMING COMEBACKS

Chapter 22

Hakuna-Matata

Twenty-nine years later, I feel pretty inspired watching the new version of the "Lion King." When I was young, I remember thinking that movie was just a sad movie about animals. Now, as a young adult in my late twenties, I have a newfound appreciation for it. The scene where Simba's dad speaks to him from the clouds and tells him to remember, that moment for Simba redirected his entire mentality and in turn, led to his successful leadership. Simba was so lost and depressed over the loss of his father and the mistakes he had made along with all the rejection that he had experienced, that he lost sight of the bigger picture. Who knew a Disney movie could be so insightful!?

When we lose someone, we allow our regrets to distort our thoughts and haunt our decisions. We beat ourselves up with regret and lose our direction in life. That was me; I was Simba. When my dad passed, I had many regrets and I let them change me. I never responded to the last text my dad sent me, that changed me. How could I have dismissed such an important message from my father!? What was I doing that was SOOOOOO important!? Why did I choose to move to L.A. when I could have been by my dad's side? Everyone told me that I shouldn't have regrets. Everyone said there was no way I could've known. Everyone said I needed to move on and live my life. But it only seemed right to feel regret, it seemed human to wish I had loved him more and hugged him more. In those moments, I didn't hear a voice from Heaven, I heard a soft whisper in my heart, "remember who you belong to my child." I am a daughter of a King. I am royalty in Heaven. Living a life of regret will only lead you down a path of destruction. The enemy wants you to be filled with regret so you are distracted from your true calling.

I had a friend who once told me that when your loved one is in Heaven, they aren't going to look down with thoughts of, "they could have been there more, what a bad daughter or son I had." The regrets we have here on earth will vanish the moment we step into our real home in Heaven. A God-designed mansion in Heaven where the streets are paved with pure gold. Our regrets are long gone, distant thoughts that no longer need to chain you down. I pray right now my friend, whatever regret that continues to haunt you, I pray that it's released. I pray for you to surrender it, lift it up and unburden your soul. Leave it where it's meant to be, in the past. You have no control of changing what has happened, the only control you have is how you think and how you act in the present. Let God's love redefine your regrets. Give it to the one who can heal you from the inside-out.

Leaving a legacy can have so many definitions. How you live your life can reflect the legacy left by your parents. What important life lessons do you want to leave instilled in the hearts of your children? For me, I want to respectfully honor the legacy that my dad left by telling his story of courageous resilience. How his pain had purpose and through God's unconditional love, my dad was able to endure every fear he faced. That his life will not be forgotten or go unnoticed, not just for him, but for everyone. Everyone has a story. Bob Goff nailed it when he said in his new book, *Dream Big* "Our ambitions should point toward the legacy we want to leave behind."

Go share and speak your truth with confidence, Hakuna Matata. It means no worries. Don't worry about anything, instead pray about everything.

Chapter 23

Quarantine

As I was working on this book, I had everything lined up for the release; speaking engagements, book signings, you name it. Little did I know, that in just a few short weeks, we as a nation, were about to face an event that would change the world and forever be a part of history. A global pandemic, COVID-19. Quarantined in houses, working from home, no social gatherings, no shaking hands, no hugs, and maintaining a distance of six feet or more from everyone around you. This was yet again, another "new" normal for me. My love language is touch. I'm all about free hugs to strangers and holding hands when I'm talking to people. So this no touchy-touch was going to be tough. I started to feel discouraged, uncertain, fearful and hopeless. Hearing all the unprecedented events occurring, hundreds of lives passing, small businesses shutting down, the loss of jobs, the loss of money, it was all mentally hard to grasp.

I started working at the call center for the COVID-19 hotline and even pondered starting to practice respiratory therapy again, since that was my original degree. Living in San Diego California, we got hit pretty bad with the virus. As I took calls through the healthcare organization, I could sense the panic, fear, and uncertainty in all the COVID patients calling in. The grief behind lost loved ones, lost jobs, and the lost normalcy of life. Simple things like grocery shopping, sporting events, and hiking along the beach suddenly nonexistent.

My mom being in the high-risk category, we had to take extra precaution. She and I were just talking the other day about what it would be like if Dad was still living at the nursing home; not being able to visit him during the lockdown. How devastating that would be. Then we began to realize, this is what the residents at nursing homes are going through RIGHT NOW. Being in lockdown for the last days of their lives and on top of that, not being able to see their loved ones or say goodbye. It really makes you think about what we take for granted.

Despite the hardships, God would never leave us without hope and without some semblance of a silver lining. Families that are always on the go and never get to spend time with one another are now able to sit around the dinner table and be present. Families are being creative together, listening to each other, cultivating their love and strength, and learning new things. I see my niece and nephew (Addison and Gabe) next door with their parents who are teaching them how to garden. I learned how to cook and clean my room with my mom for the first time in twenty-nine years (I know, I know). We, as a nation, watched Easter for the first time online. That was different, but hey, who says different is bad? Different is just... different. With change comes growth, just like we've talked about before. The world got a reset and trust me, nature needed it. The air is more crisp and pure, the symphony of birds more harmonious, the sky more clear from the lack of traffic (and in L.A. this is such a blessing, you have no idea...), everything just seems to be...happier. It got me thinking about our family trip to Yosemite after my dad passed. Every morning, on the deck of our vacation home, there was a blue jay that came to visit. We started to feed him and at the time, I was so detached from the beauty around me I couldn't see the sign that I do now. I think my dad was trying to give us a little "hello" from above. Blue was his favorite color. My favorite one and only niece Addison even made up a song dedicated to the little birdie, "blue jay, blue jay, how are you today." We will only see what we want to see. If you can only see the negative, then that's all you'll see. But if you can open your heart, your eyes, and your mind to the beauty that is, life will be much more enjoyable, you'll see.

I've been taking walks regularly now with my mom, something new we've been doing to get some fresh air. Sometimes Addison and Gabe would join us, as I look to either side of me, my heart smiles. I am truly rich and all I need has always been right here. Family, faith and love. It's all we need.

So, during this time instead of feeling discouraged and trapped with heightened emotions or thoughts like, I'm turning 30 in a few months and I need to get my book published blah, blah, blah...try to see what you *do* have and be grateful for it. When we think or feel like something is coming to an end, fear takes hold and we lose track of what's truly important. This could be the end of our time on earth, I mean, we will never really know until it happens. But our final destination doesn't just stop here, we have a paradise in Heaven that is ready and waiting. I can't help but think of my dad more than ever during this time. He would know exactly just what to say. Remember my friend, we don't know what the future holds, but we know *who* holds the future. What may seem like a setback, can and will become your biggest comeback #Trust #Believe and never give up!

Now it's time for me to go wash my hands for 20 seconds…

Chapter 24

It's Just the Beginning

Our end is HIS beginning. Believe that.

"It's okay, Danny, close your eyes, rest. Rest your eyes. I'm here. We are all here."

After forty-three years of marriage, those were the final words spoken by my mom as she gently laid my dad to rest, one last time. It was June 13th, 2018. Firmly united in spirit, we stood around that hospital bed, as a family, alongside our hero. We sang songs while tears flowed down and hugged him as he walked through Heaven's golden gates. A few months after my dad's celebration of life, I had met up with a family friend who attended the service. She had told me something that brought me to tears. When she went to my dad's service, she had no faith, she had no relationship with God. But after leaving that service, after witnessing our fellowship and feeling something she had never felt before, she decided she wanted that. She wanted that "thing" whatever it was. That "thing" we had was hope. Knowing that when you lose a loved one it's never goodbye. Hope for an eternal life. That evening, she went to a church and dedicated her life to God by accepting Jesus into her heart. God works in mysterious ways, my friend. We don't have to live with facts or answers. All we need is faith.

We had an inspiration jar, where everyone who attended my dad's celebration of life would write a small note of how he inspired them. I like to read the notes on the days I'm feeling a little down; on the days I need a spicy, siracha kick in the butt. Reading the notes reminds me of the impact my dad had on so many people. That God was able to use my dad's disability as a powerful tool for teaching. My dad showed the world, that though his life was cut short at sixty-three years old, he accomplished exactly what he was meant to accomplish. He inspired, he loved, and he encouraged, all in the name of Jesus. Through JESUS, anything is possible. No disability, addiction, grief, loss, heartache or pain is ever too much for Jesus to handle.

I remember every moment of that day. Every. Single. Moment. I remember the doctors walking in at 6:30 p.m. with a demeanor of calm respect, acknowledging what was about to happen behind the curtain. I was so scared. I had never witnessed someone dying before my eyes and now, my twenty-seven-year old body had to withstand witnessing my father leaving this world. I was not ready. We were not ready. You won't be ready. No one will ever be ready no matter how prepared you think you may be. I remember wearing the same shirt for two weeks straight; it said "Worlds. Best. Dad. Ever." It was a shirt I had gotten for him to wear, on what turned out to be, his last Father's Day. I remember closing my swollen, dry eyes, fresh-out-of-tears, holding his left hand and using it to cover my ear—protecting me one more time.

What I couldn't recognize at the time was the truth that was holding onto my soul. The truth in knowing I wasn't alone. We are never alone. God didn't promise us a pain-free life, but He did promise that he would never leave us.

My cousin, Elizabeth, whom I call "sister," flew from Arizona to San Diego the second she found out what happened. She didn't comfort me with her words. I was in such a state of shock that words didn't even make sense. But she did comfort me with her presence. If there's any advice I can give to people about helping others through grief, it's just to be there. Allow them to speak, cry out and tell stories. Be a shoulder for them to cry on. Don't try to give advice because you don't know, you can't know, unless you've experienced it yourself. Just listen and show up for those that are grieving. We call it the ministry of presence.

My cousin didn't say much, but what she did say, I'll hold onto forever. As I held my dad's lifeless hand, she said to me softly, "Hannah, your dad right now is standing outside the gates of Heaven. He's looking down, laughing and smiling at his daughter, confused as to why she's crying. Your dad is having a long conversation with God asking, 'Why is my daughter crying when I'm perfectly fine.' Your dad was so excited and ready to stand up from his wheelchair and walk through those gates." She was right. I looked around, across the hall at the very room where I was born. The irony of birth and death. I was the last one to accept that my dad was not leaving this third floor hospital room. I was the last one to comprehend that there was nothing else the doctors could have done. I meditated on her words as I watched the heart monitor slowly decline. Number by number, while I listened to my dad's breathing slow to a soft murmur. It was weird for me to watch his vitals go down and not have nurses running or MD's recommending something while my family frantically watched on, helplessly. This time we surrendered his life to God, trusting and believing that my dad was now pain free and standing in the presence of the Lord in a twinkle of an eye. Every unanswered prayer, doubt, fear, and disability washed away by the breath of God as my dad took his first step into paradise. I envision my sweet, strong dad standing up with confidence, laughing and breathing in the freshest air with new lungs, new life, and new energy as the angels sing their praise.

How foreign, yet somehow, comforting it was, to know that the moment I saw the flatline of his heartbeat, that my iron man, my dad, was no longer in pain. He accomplished exactly what God intended for him, for sixty-three resilient years. He walked that narrow path in life, endured the race, and he finished well.

My friend, as you move through this life, there will be moments you fall, moments where you question your existence, value, character, and purpose. Acknowledge that pain. Grieve and accept the emotions that come with it. For me, that meant crying in my room every single day for one year, and that's okay. IT'S OKAY, TO NOT BE OKAY. Those tough moments where I allowed myself to cry and be real, that's when I started to heal. IN ORDER TO HEAL, YOU NEED TO BE REAL.

Embrace the unknown and gracefully allow the fresh flow of new hope into your soul with arms held high in complete surrender. You are loved. You are seen. You are valuable. We don't know our plans or what the future holds, but we know that God has plans for us. The best is yet to come.

What is life? Life is embracing joy in the unknown. It's using your pain for purpose. It's allowing transformational hope to heal your wounds and build that resilience. It's trusting in God and remembering His love for you. It's living a life full of love and purpose. My friend, it's been an honor and privilege to have had you join me on this journey. May peace surpass all your understanding and refresh your soul.

My hope and prayer is that you were able to witness the power of Jesus through this book. That right now, wherever you are, you have decided to accept the invitation to eternal life. Paradise awaits us all in Heaven. Pray this life changing prayer and get ready for a purposeful life worth living.

Kindly repeat these words in your heart, "Dear Lord Jesus, I am tired of living the way I've been. I know that I have turned my back against you. I acknowledge I am sinner. I ask for Your forgiveness. I believe you died for my sins and rose from the dead. I'm inviting you into my heart to change my life. I want to trust and follow you as my Lord and Savior all the rest of my days. Write my name in the Lamb's Book of Life. In Jesus name, AMEN."

Congratulations! You just made the best decision ever! Your name is now written in the Lamb's Book of Life, which means, Heaven is your eternal home. The end of this book has now become your beginning, a new fulfilled life my sweet brother or sister in Christ. We are family now.

> *"This means that anyone who belongs to Christ has become a new person. The old life is gone; a new life has begun!"*
>
> (2 CORINTHIANS 5:17 NLT)

Dad, this was for you. I'm endlessly grateful and honored to call you my dad, my iron man. Our special bond is never over, it's always forever. It's *Never Goodbye*, just see ya later! My guardian angel, I love you, MAHAL KITA. Forever your princess daughter. #GirlDad

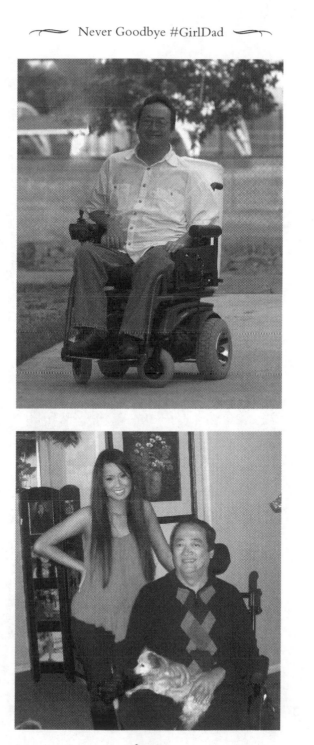

"*My Dearest Hannah,*
May you have a wonderful fun birthday today. Thank you for your love
and cheering me up for the last 24yrs, even in my most difficult times.
Remember to always look up to the man above for wisdom and guidance.
This will be your key to success and full filling your dreams. I am so
blessed and you are treasure that God sent to me. Love you my Princess,
Dad"

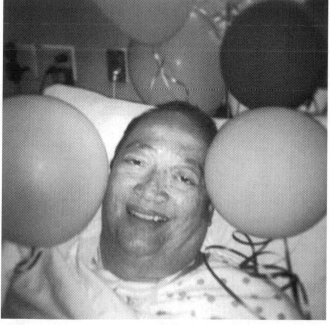

Afterword

"Dr. Joya embraced a key ingredient to a successful life, he had persistence and grace. He did what he could with what he had, where he was and he always did it with a smile."

It is my honor to have read *Never Goodbye #GirlDad* written by daughter Hannah Joya. The book is a spiritual love story between father, daughter and family. She describes the pain, grief, anxiety, depression and struggle of how she managed. At the same time her father stood as an example that helped her and all who knew him.

Losing someone we love and admire is an emotional experience where we may be forced to face our own values and personal mortality. The detailed account by Hannah describes her growth and development in a loving family with a father who faced numerous challenges. She articulates an emotional connection to her family and to her faith. During this era of Covid19 there will be many families who can relate to this, as pointed out by Hannah. The measure of how we handle these challenges define us. This book will give the pathway that Hannah and her family took. How Hannah helped her family, cared for her father and selected a career is thoughtfully described in her roadmap.

I had the honor of working with Dr. Danny Joya and learning from him. He came into my office quadriplegic in a wheel chair with a smiling face and whispering voice. He wanted to work in our Pulmonary and Sleep Division. At the time I was Emeritus Medical Director of the Viterbi Family Scripps Clinic Sleep Center. He was a physician but no longer could practice because of his illness. He wanted to do something but was not sure what was possible. He did not ask to be paid but only wanted to do something *meaningful*. We often had visiting physicians work with us but never someone quadriplegic. Dr. Joya's desire clearly came across and I discussed this with my colleagues. With the help of Dr.Dan Kripke, a major leading physician scientist in our group we thought of a project. With the outline of Dr. Kripke and the effort of Dr. Joya he reviewed numerous papers and data from several pharmaceutical companies to determine the risk of infection for patients taking hypnotics. Amazingly he accumulated a large database and ultimately a publication where Dr. Joya was the lead author. This article has been cited in in the scientific and public literature over 52 times, an example that many people thought his work was very meaningful.

(Joya, F.L., Kripke, D.F., Loving, R.T., Dawson, A., and Kline, L.E. Meta-Analyses of Hypnotics and Infections: Eszopiclone, Ramelteon, Zaleplon, and Zolpidem. J.Clin.Sleep Med. 5(4), 377-383. 2009).

Seeing Dr. Joya work with his substantial limitations and observing him participate in our conferences and meetings was impressive. His effort to write the manuscript was amazing. We all learned from what he was able to do. Dr. Joya embraced a key ingredient to a *successful* life, he had **persistence** and **grace**. He did what he could with what he had, where he was and he always did it with a smile. A lesson for us all. He loved people and his family and he was loved. *How would you like to be remembered?*

-**Lawrence E. Kline, DO, FACP, FCCP, FAASM**
Associate Professor of Medicine
Division of Pulmonary, Critical
Care and Sleep Medicine
University of California San Diego

Acknowledgements

Thiiis book wouldn't even have been considered if it wasn't for the desire placed in my heart by the one who goes before me and loves me unconditionally, Jesus. Thank you for giving me a story to tell and thank you for blessing me with a life that is nourished by faith. I've tried to live without you, but time and time again, I'm reminded that it just ain't livable. Living my life by your exemplary love is my sole mission.

My dad, my "iron man," no words can truly express the magnitude of love we have for each other. Nothing can compare to the instrumental role you had in my life and the sacrifices you consistently made for the sake of our family. I am forever grateful and honored to have had a dad like you. My life now and who I have become was molded by your influence; everything you taught me has become an integral part of who I am. To be given twenty-seven years with a dad like you was truly a gift; a gift that brought me purpose in this life. Your legacy and love will forever live through me and this book. I dedicate everything this book is, has become, and will be, to you and God. Until we meet again in sweet paradise, I'll use the pain to fuel my purpose. I love you always. #GirlDad

To my sweet and devoted mother, who consistently gets mistaken as my younger, twin sister, this book wouldn't have even crossed my mind if it wasn't for your fierce love and encouragement. Your words were the inspiration behind the writing. Thank you for always reminding me that I never had to chase my purpose and story; that I was already living it. Thank you for being my solid foundation, my constant cheerleader and the heart of our family. You are the woman I strive to become. Just as Dad played a vital part in the person I am, so did you. I am who I am today, because of you. My best friend, my role model, I love you Mom.

To all my Aunties: Auntie Maggie, Auntie Martha, and Auntie Marcela. Thank you for being the best sisters to my mom and always being there for me in more ways than I could've ever imagined. Thanks for all the beautiful dresses you found at stores that you knew I'd love, for supporting me through comments and likes on my social media platforms, for cheering me on at soccer games, and bringing food to the hospitals/nursing homes. But most importantly, thank you for never allowing me to feel alone; you all have been there and kept me going. I love you my amazing Aunties. My Halmoni (Korean Grandmother), for being the prayer warrior in our family.

Virginia, you were the first to lay eyes on my words. You were the one reassuring me that my dad never left my side through all the sweat and tears that went into this book. I remember when we first met years ago, you brought my dad companionship in a time of need. Seeing you both sitting in the lobby at the nursing home brought so much comfort to my heart in knowing that you had each other. You've loved our family like your own. Your editing eye is what started this book off in the right direction. Thank you so much. I have been so blessed to have you by my side from the beginning until the end; you are forever family to me.

Annalisa, my manuscript fairy queen. I can't even begin to tell you how grateful I am to have you. Thank you for bringing sparkle and shine to my words and for simply "getting it." All of my emotions and hope written on paper, you brought to life. Having you edit my work in the heart of your own grief…it just shows how perfectly timed God's plan can be. I know both of our dads are standing together in paradise, so proud of what we got through together. Thank you and beyond.

Chelcea, my graphic designer. You were the only one who saw my vision for the front and back cover. You always believed in me. I remember when I first showed you the image I wanted to use, after everyone else had said it was too dehumanizing, but no, not you. You heard me. You saw the impact that picture could have before anyone else did. In your unwavering patience, you helped to propel me towards success. I'm so glad our dads got to meet each other in Heaven.

Westbow Press, thank you for being a part of this new journey. The book world was so unfamiliar to me, but from the beginning your staff brought so much reassurance, organization and quality to my work. Thank you for providing me with the best team to help me accomplish, through God's power, my first book ever. I'm so grateful, from the bottom of my heart, for everything.

To all the physicians and medical staff who provided extra ordinary care and love for my dad, the world needs more people like you. Words can't express my gratitude for extending my father's life for twenty-seven more years of love and laughter. Thank you.

Austen, thanks for being my chill pill and believing in me as I wrote this book. Thank you for listening to my out-loud, late night readings and reminding me that this is what I was meant to do.

And last but not least, to all my family and friends that weren't named specifically, the list is so long, but ya'll know who ya'll are. I wouldn't be here today without your constant affirmations, love, and support. From the beginning of my life until now, you all were there to remind me of God's goodness. Thank you for always encouraging my dad as he battled twenty-seven years of illness. Thank you, thank you, and thank you. I'm forever grateful to do this life with each and every one of you.

About the Author

Hannah Joya, born and raised in sunny San Diego, California, made a promise to tell the world about her Father's life story. In 2018 her Dad's life was cut short after his battle with GBS-CIDP (Guillain Barre Syndrome-Chronic Inflammatory Demyelinating Polyneuropathy), a chronic and progressive condition where the body essentially attacks itself, causing permanent nerve damage over time. At the age of twenty-nine, her dreams finally became a reality. Being able to tell the story about her Father's perseverance, his mentality, his can-do and will-do attitude and his fight until the very end, has always been close to her heart.

She was a firsthand witness to all the struggles and joy of her Father's journey. There is no doubt that Hannah's support system comes from the family that surrounds her; their strength fuels her strength and continues to be a driving factor in her life. Her family once organized the first 5K Run to support the GBS-CIDP foundation held in San Diego and ended up raising enough funds to exceed any set expectations and help fuel further research into this debilitating disease.

Hannah lived in a world where the only vision of her Father she had ever known was of him confined to a wheelchair. She never had the privilege of seeing him walk, run, swim or dance, but that didn't stop her from living life to the fullest for her father and eventually for herself. Her passion for helping others transpired into various volunteer opportunities all over the San Diego area. She joined a peace team in 2017 with Saddleback Church to assist in bringing relief to hurricane Harvey victims and worked with several outreach programs that focused on serving the homeless community. She also volunteered at numerous elder and assisted living communities alongside her Mom who is the community ambassador of the Assisted Living Ministry. Bringing joy to people who often times feel they have been forgotten. Her active engagement within her church has led to successful mission trips to orphanages in Mexico and she plans to continue to help those in need in any way she can.

Hannah is currently a model and an actress. She was Miss North County San Diego in 2016 and has been featured in numerous campaigns for name brand beauty/clothing lines along with nationwide commercials. Having received a degree in respiratory therapy, she chose a career path as a marketing coordinator and works at one of the top hospitals in San Diego

County. Today, Hannah resides in San Diego to be close to family and friends where her inspiration originated.

Her true source of happiness is to inspire those around her and help them cope with pain, loss, and heartache. In helping people understand that behind sorrow lies purpose and finding hope in hopeless moments. Her mission is to keep her Dad's legacy alive and with this book, she plans to do just that.

Stay connected on social media
Instagram: hannahmariejoya
Facebook: Hannah Joya

Printed in the United States
By Bookmasters